Persuasive Interviewing

Persuasive Interviewing

A Forensic Case Analysis

Don Rabon
Tanya Chapman

CAROLINA ACADEMIC PRESS
Durham, North Carolina

Library of Congress Cataloging-in-Publication Data

Rabon, Don.
  Persuasive interviewing / by Don Rabon, Tanya Chapman.
    p. cm.
  Includes bibliographical references and index.
  ISBN-13: 978-1-59460-367-9 (alk. paper)
  ISBN-10: 1-59460-367-7 (alk. paper)
  1. Interviewing in law enforcement--United States. 2. Police questioning--United States. 3. Persuasion (Psychology) I. Chapman, Tanya. II. Title.

  HV8073.3.R33 2007
  363.25'4--dc22   2007006462

Carolina Academic Presss
700 Kent St.
Durham, NC 27701
Telephone (919) 489-7486
Fax (919) 493-5668
www.cap-press.com

Printed in the United States of America

Contents

Preface

This text and its parallel materials are designed for broad-based application and utilization. The experienced interviewer and those new to the persuasion process, as it relates to interviewing and interrogation, will find the opportunity to develop and enhance their persuasive skills. In addition to the text an Instructor Manual and a Student Workbook are also available. These additional resources lend themselves to the presentation of the materials in a practitioner training setting, as well as an academic environment. Lastly, working through all the elements of the materials will enhance the knowledge, skills, and abilities of the experienced interviewer.

The Student Workbook contains content related exercises and an examination for each chapter. The Instructor Manual contains answers to the Application Exercises, examinations and supporting information for the text. A familiarity with the material found in the texts *Interviewing and Interrogation* and *Investigative Discourse Analysis,* (by Don Rabon, Carolina Academic Press, 1992 and 1994) would be of benefit but is not a prerequisite.

The primary concentration of the text is the breakdown, examination, and evaluation of the last eighteen minutes of an eighty-minute homicide interview. We will study specifically what the interviewer incorporated into his verbal (involving words) and vocal (including sounds and silence) communication to persuade the interviewee to acquiesce. The goal is to learn not just what transpired but also why and how.

The chapters include explanatory notes placed within the examined transcript that help the reader understand exactly what transpires during the interview. The careful analysis of the persuasive methods and strategy applied by the interviewer enables the reader to acquire these skills and incorporate them into his or her own persuasive communication skill set.

There are application questions and an "Application Exercise" located in the accompanying Student Workbook, allowing the reader to pause and reflect on the material and how it can relate to their own persuasive responsibilities. The related activities are designed to reinforce the presented material. These exercises allow the reader to apply what has previously been presented in a broader context, enhancing the learning process and laying the foundation for improved persuasive communication skills.

As a result, the experienced persuader may work through the text and supporting materials rather quickly, not needing to pause, contemplate, and apply but rather moving steadily to the end of the journey, picking up interesting and applicable pieces of information along the way. The apprentice, however, may want to slow down, reflect, and even backtrack along the trails and take a look at some of the elements more than once. For the experienced traveler it is the destination that is most important. For those new to the experience it is the journey itself that is most important. Hopefully for both, this text will serve as a useful vehicle and the excursion will be of benefit to one and all.

Lastly, persons responsible for the delivery of information and the development of skills in others will find this material a valuable resource. The level of instruction can range from basic to advanced.

As always when conducting interviews of this nature, follow the legal parameters that are prescribed within your jurisdiction, the organizational policy and procedure related to interviewing, and the preferential criteria of the local prosecuting authority.

Acknowledgment

Bill and Nancy; Don and Rachel

Persuasive Interviewing

Chapter One

Persuasion — It's All About Communication

When the conduct of men is designed to be influenced, persuasion, kind unassuming persuasion, should ever be adopted. It is an old and true maxim that 'a drop of honey catches more flies than a gallon of gall.' So with men. If you would win a man to your cause, first convince him that you are his sincere friend. Therein is a drop of honey that catches his heart, which, say what he will, is the great highroad to his reason, and which, once gained, you will find but little trouble in convincing him of the justice of your cause, if indeed that cause is really a good one.

Abraham Lincoln (1809–1865)

Of the three operational elements of the interview process—questioning, detecting deception, and persuasion, the most problematic, enigmatic, and complex is the third—the concept of persuasion. At the outset of the interview, the primary question in the mind of the interviewer who is faced with the challenge of motivating someone to do something they have no intention of doing is "How? How can I, through my communication undertakings, motivate this individual to do what I want him to do?"

Certainly this third element is going to be the primary focus of a challenge within the judicial process as it relates to the interview—"What did you do, through your interview (communication undertakings), to my client that caused him to make an admission?" Being prepared to defend and articulate the persuasive process that results in a confession in open court is a constant challenge for anyone who regularly interviews.

At the very least the persuasion process is difficult. Each interviewee is different from any other interviewee ever encountered before. Motives and emotions all combine to ensure there is no one-size-fits-all persuasion strategy—one that simply starts at one point and ends at another, with the interviewee simply on the conveyer belt, ending up cooperating and having no influence over the outcome or his own fate.

3

Nevertheless, cooperation does in fact happen. Interviewees cooperate and confess on a fairly consistent basis. We simply want to have the cooperation happen more often so we as interviewers strive to function with ever-increasing effectiveness. Now the question is "Why? Why would someone do something seemingly against their own self interest?" Well, if we can answer that—and we can—then we are well on our way to answering the first question, "How?"

So, together we will explore and examine the persuasion process. We will travel from antiquity to the present, discovering throughout the passage of time that the constant and the variable are the same—it is all about people, and why they do what they do, and how it is possible to motivate them to go in the direction the interviewer has in mind.

The First Interview Resulting in a Behavioral Change

As noted above, we are going to start at square one. And while our examination of interviews as communication-persuasive events will encounter some attempts to change behavior that are lengthier than this, the process will never become more complex or more successful than the following:

"*1Now the serpent was more subtile than any beast of the field which the LORD God had made. And he said unto the woman, Yea, hath God said, Ye shall not eat of every tree of the garden? 2And the woman said unto the serpent, We may eat of the fruit of the trees of the garden: 3but of the fruit of the tree which is in the midst of the garden, God hath said, Ye shall not eat of it, neither shall ye touch it, lest ye die. 4And the serpent said unto the woman, Ye shall not surely die: 5for God doth know that in the day ye eat thereof, then your eyes shall be opened, and ye shall be as gods, knowing good and evil. 6And when the woman saw that the tree was good for food, and that it was pleasant to the eyes, and a tree to be desired to make one wise, she took of the fruit thereof, and did eat, and gave also unto her husband with her; and he did eat.*"

Genesis 3:1–6

Everything we need to understand with regard to the persuasion process takes places in these short six verses. Within the persuasive interview our communication is designed to affect the cognitive process of the interviewee. Stated simply, we want to influence the behavioral outcome of the interviewee by guiding his thinking (cognition). In order to affect another person's behavior we have to first get their attention and then we have to make them imagine it—make them think. In both of these two dynamics we use our communication skills to succeed.

Application Question: How do we get someone's attention?

A most effectual strategy for gaining someone's attention is the utilization of questions. The first communication act on the part of the serpent (the first persuader) is to ask Eve a question:

> *"Yea, hath God said, Ye shall not eat of every tree of the garden?"*

Questions activate the cognitive process. In order to respond to the Serpent's question, Eve has to think first and then answer:

> *"… We may eat of the fruit of the trees of the garden: ³but of the fruit of the tree which is in the midst of the garden, God hath said, Ye shall not eat of it, neither shall ye touch it, lest ye die."*

At this point, her barrier to cooperation (behavior change) has been brought forth, and the serpent is now in a position address her concern:

> *"… Ye shall not surely die: ⁵for God doth know that in the day ye eat thereof, then your eyes shall be opened, and ye shall be as gods, knowing good and evil."*

Now all of the dynamics are in place: the serpent has gained her attention through a question, Eve has articulated her concern, and the serpent has countered her concern.

All that remains is for the wheels which have been set in motion to run their course. Eve has to process the information communicated to her, make the decision (to change her mind), and provide the behavioral outcome planned by the serpent all along:

> *"… ⁶And when the woman saw that the tree was good for food, and that it was pleasant to the eyes, and a tree to be desired to make one wise, she took of the fruit thereof, and did eat,…"*

Eve "saw"—she thought, she came to understand, and she acted.

All along, Eve had the capacity to change her mind. The objective of the serpent was to cause her to use that capacity to bring about the behavior change he desired. Also Eve had the capacity **not** to change her mind. At the end of the day, she did not have to respond to the influential communication undertakings of the serpent. And these are two important elements to keep in mind as we proceed in our study: the interviewee is capable of change, and that change has to be voluntary. We, as ethical interviewers, do not want to take away the "free will" aspect of the persuasion process. If the cooperation (confession) is not a function of free will, then a false confession by an innocent person becomes a distinct possibility. A false confession is not what we want. We are seeking the truth. How ironic it is that we start our study with an examination of the tactics used by the "Father of Lies" in order to better know how to obtain the truth.

Exercise 1, Chapter 1

Turn to Appendix A and thoroughly read the interview transcript. Knowing fully what has transpired prior to the final eighteen minutes of the transcript is important to our study.

Questions to Address with Regard to Persuasion

As we begin our study with regard to the persuasion process, we will address the related terms, concepts, and definitions. As with any study, learning the associated vocabulary is half of the journey.

Note: As you address these questions, first think about what the terms mean to you before you read a formal definition. Remember the persuasion process is as much about you in some aspects (as the interviewer) as it is about the interviewee.

Application Question: What is persuasion?

"A process of inducing a person to adopt a particular set of values, beliefs or attitudes."[1]

The interviewer as a persuader is tasked with *inducing* the interviewee to *adopt* a new mindset. In order for this to happen the interviewee has to change. He has to take upon himself—accept something he previously had not accepted. According to this definition he has to change either:
- set of values;
- beliefs;
- attitudes;
or a combination thereof.

Application Question: What does it mean to induce?

"To cause or bring about a thought, feeling or physical condition."[2]

The interviewer is an agent of change. For the persuasion process to be successful, the interviewee has to transition from a mindset of non-cooperation to cooperation. Consequently, the communicative behavior of the interviewer is directed toward the accomplishment of that goal.

Application Question: What are values?

"… the patterns of behavior within a particular culture or society which, through the process of socialization, the members of that culture or society hold in high regard."[3]

The resulting application questions for the interviewer include:
- What values does this individual possess?
- What or who does this individual hold in "high regard?" (The persons and/or things held in high regard are known as the individual's "subjective norm.")
- How will this individual's values help or hinder the persuasion process?

Application Question: What are beliefs?

"… an emotional acceptance of some proposition, statement or doctrine".[4]

So we come to understand that emotions play a role within the persuasion process. The interviewee has an "emotional acceptance" of some dynamic that can either be an assistance or obstruction to the persuasion process. That dynamic as it applies to the persuasion process—meaning the propositions the interviewer might possibly employ—could include: personal responsibility, rationalization, shifting the blame, it was too great a temptation, we all make mistakes, etc.

Application Question: What are attitudes?

"Some internal affective orientation that would explain the actions of a person … entails several components, namely: cognitive (consciously held belief or opinion); affective (emotional tone or feeling); evaluative (positive or negative); and conative (disposition for action)."[5]

The interviewee brings a set of personal attitudes with him into the interview event. His attitudes are learned, and they tend to stay with him throughout life. The interviewee's attitudes determine, in no small part, his subsequent behavior.

Exercise 2, Chapter 1

Having laid the foundation for the persuasion process, we will utilize the remaining portion of the transcript as a learning vehicle. Read the following portion of the transcript thoroughly. Throughout this book you will see the abbreviations **IR** and **IE**. **IR** represents statements made or questions asked by the interviewer, **IE** represents those made by interviewee.

847 IR: OK. Now Andrew, I'm going to lay this on the line to you.

848 IE: OK.

849 IR: You've been talking now for almost an hour, forty minutes.

850 IE: Well, I was just trying to be as cooperative …

851 IR: No. And I appreciate that. There's going to be an autopsy tomorrow.
852   And I have already seen the x-rays and the scan. I have a pretty good
853   idea of what happened to the baby. OK. There's been a lot of science
854   done over the years about what injuries cause what to babies. You
855   know what I'm saying?

856 IE: Yeah.

857 IR: We can medically say. We can date bruises, date cuts. We can date
858   breaks in bones.

859 IE: OK.

860 IR: All of these.

861 IE: I don't I don't believe she had anything like that.

862 IR: OK. But we can scientifically do that.

863 IE: Right.

864 IR: OK. And that's going to be done one way or the other. Eventually this
865   is going to go, this situation, the whole deal, three days is going to go
866   to a district attorney. OK. And the district attorney is going to sit down
867   and listen to all the facts. And you've told your side of the story. We've
868   got Ann's story. We've got the autopsy. So we've got a lot of different
869   stories. OK. And if several of the stories match and one of them doesn't,
870   how do you think the DA is going to view that?

871 IE: I don't know. The thing that I'm telling you, you know, is true.

872 IR: OK. And that's what I want.

873 IE: The fall is, you know, that, that happened.

874 IR: OK. And I want you to tell the truth. I don't want you to tell me any-
875   thing that didn't happen.

876 IE: That's, that's what happened.

877 IR: OK. The DA is going to make a decision that can affect the rest of your
878   life.

879 IE: Right.

880 IR: Because they're going to decide whether to charge you with murder,
881   whether to charge you with child abuse resulting in death, whether
882   to charge you with negligence, whether to charge you with man-
883   slaughter, second degree murder or maybe nothing. See there are a
884   lot of options out there for the district attorney.

885 IE: Right.

886 IR: Now, first degree murder carries what? Do you know?

887 IE: No.

888 IR: That's a life sentence. That's mandatory life. We can go all the way down
889   to negligence which carries a few years. Or even child abuse, misde-
890   meanor child abuse which carries you know it's a misdemeanor term. OK.

891 IE: OK.

892 IR: OK. So it's a very important decision that the DA is going to make. OK.
893   Whatever decision he makes it's going to go onto court. Right? Unless
894   they don't charge you with anything.

895 IE: Right.

896 IR: OK. It's going to go onto court probably and there'll be a case. And
897   eventually that case will go before twelve people in a jury.

898 IE: Right.

899 IR: Right. And those twelve people are going to get to see this tape. They
900   are going to get to see what you said. How that you held the baby and
901   all those kinds of things.

902 IE: That's, that's totally fine.

903 IR: Right.

904 IE: 'Cause everything that I told you is true.

905 IR: OK.

906 IE: And that's, that's the way it happened.

907 IR: OK. And here's what I want to tell you, Andrew.

908 IE: OK.

909 IR: OK. What you are telling me doesn't add up. And so what they're
910   going to hear is just that.

911 IE: What do you mean it doesn't add up?

912 IR: I'm going to explain that to you.

913 IE: OK.

914 IR: What I want you to think about is this. If you were one of those twelve
915   people and somebody else was sitting there in front of you, would you
916   rather hear from them, "Ah, hey, it was an accident. I didn't mean for
917   it to happen this way. I lost my temper. I'm not that kind of a guy. I
918   would never intentionally hurt a child. I might have just got frustrated
919   for a second."

920 IE: No.

921 IR: No. I'm just telling you. I want you to think about it.

922 IE: I don't get frustrated.

923 IR: I want you to think about it.

924 IE: OK.

Breakdown—Analysis of the Transcript and the Persuasion Process Segment One

Now that we have read this portion of the transcript, we will begin our systematic examination of exactly what persuasion dynamics have taken place during this segment.

847 IR: OK. Now Andrew, I'm going to lay this on the line to you.

848 IE: OK.

Note: This is the transitional point within the interview process. Up to this point, all of the interview has been involved in information gathering, confirming previously known or suspected information, and allowing the interviewee to give his presentation by way of his narrative and his responses to the interviewer's questions. We will refer to this phase as the "Green Zone." At this junction the goal shifts from information gathering to subtle information presentation. This segment is now concerned with the initial steps of the "process of inducing." The objective now is to lay the foundation that will enable the interviewer to persuade. It is important to note that the process of inducing is not necessarily "the process of telling." Cognition precedes a change in behavior, and one of the best devices for inducing cognition is asking questions. We are still within the Green Zone but pay attention, the color code can change very quickly.

Coaching Points:
- Let the subject present his narrative;
- Do not demonstrate any indication of disbelief;
- Based upon the information you carry into the interview, structure your questions in a manner that will cause the interviewee to establish himself in line with or in opposition to what you already know.

849 IR: You've been talking now for almost an hour, forty minutes.

850 IE: Well, I was just trying to be as cooperative …

851 IR: No. And I appreciate that. There's going to be an autopsy tomorrow.

852   And I have already seen the x-rays and the scan. I have a pretty good

853   idea of what happened to the baby. OK. There's been a lot of science

854   done over the years about what injuries cause what to babies. You

855   know what I'm saying?

856 IE: Yeah.

857 IR: We can medically say. We can date bruises, date cuts. We can date

858   breaks in bones.

859 IE: OK.

860 IR: All of these.

861 IE: I don't I don't believe she had anything like that.

862 IR: OK. But we can scientifically do that.

863 IE: Right.

Note: In lines 849–863 the interviewer has highlighted:
- the time the interviewee has had to speak;
- indications of the evidence at hand and;
- implied there is a theory as to what has occurred.

He further establishes his position by indicating that "*science*" is playing a role in the development of the theory. He begins the tentative attempt to gauge the interviewee's willingness to accept what he is asserting and to proceed, by asking simply, *"You know what I'm saying?"* Note how the interviewer has begun to apply the pronoun *"we."* The phrase *"we can"* is repeated to strengthen the assertion. This collective pronoun usage not only helps to strengthen his assertions, but also brings the concept of a nearness in relationship into his presentation. An emphasis here on the use of the pronoun "you" would only serve to widen the gap that inherently exists between the interviewer and the interviewee. *"We"* serves to bring them both together and is meant to cause the interviewee to perceive a shared experience as they move forward.

Coaching Points

- Establish a connection between yourself and the interviewee.
- Avoid building a gap through the overuse of pronouns like "you."
- Use pronouns that are more conducive to gaining cooperation.

864 IR: OK. And that's going to be done one way or the other. Eventually this
865   is going to go, this situation, the whole deal, three days is going to go
866   to a district attorney. OK. And the district attorney is going to sit down
867   and listen to all the facts. And you've told your side of the story. We've
868   got Ann's story. We've got the autopsy. So we've got a lot of different
869   stories. OK. And if several of the stories match and one of them doesn't,
870   how do you think the DA is going to view that?

Note: Between lines 864 and 870, the interviewer continues to lay out the foundational components of the as yet undisclosed theory. Then in line 870 the first cognition-inducing question is presented: *"... how do you think the DA (District Attorney) is going to view that?"* Questions cause others to think. They activate the cognitive process. Cognition precedes behavior. As Proverbs 23:7 (King James Version) states: "For as he thinketh in his heart, so is he...." The interviewer strives to guide the thinking of the interviewee to the desired conclusion—cooperation. Had the interviewer told the interviewee *"what"* the DA was going to think, it could have caused the individual to seek to terminate the interview (invoke Fifth Amendment rights for example), or to refute the supposed conclusions of the DA. By making the point through the use of a question, what the DA is going to think is now planted in the mind of the interviewee. He imagines it. The possibility of him refuting what his own cognition has brought forth is much less than if the DA's thoughts were articulated by the interviewer.

Coaching Point
- Use questions to make your point.
- Watch and listen to the interviewee carefully as you ask the question, as he processes the question, and as he answers the question.

Note: As communicators, most people only hear a portion of what is being said. Interviewers must attend on a significantly higher level. They must attend with their eyes and their ears. Always establish good eye contact with the interviewee. Do not succumb to the temptation to look at the case folder.

871 IE: I don't know. The thing that I'm telling you, you know, is true.

872 IR: OK. And that's what I want.

873 IE: The fall is, you know, that, that happened.

874 IR: OK. And I want you to tell the truth. I don't want you to tell me any-
875   thing that didn't happen.

876 IE: That's, that's what happened.

877 IR: OK. The DA is going to make a decision that can affect the rest of your
878   life.

879 IE: Right.

880 IR: Because they're going to decide whether to charge you with murder,
881   whether to charge you with child abuse resulting in death, whether
882   to charge you with negligence, whether to charge you with man-
883   slaughter, second degree murder or maybe nothing. See there are a
884   lot of options out there for the district attorney.

885 IE: Right.

Note: Between lines 871 and 885 the interviewer has delineated a series of "frames"and initiated the concept of framing: "[A]ny social situation can be defined in terms of basic principles that affect and control the ways in which people involve themselves with and experience it. These definitions are frames."[6] Framing is "[A] cognitive heuristic in which people tend to reach conclusions based on the 'framework' within which a situation is presented."[7]

By way of illustration: the interviewer has presented the following concepts (frames):
- child abuse resulting in death;
- negligence;

- manslaughter;
- second degree murder;
- nothing.

In presenting the different frames, the interviewer is attempting to find a frame in which the interviewee can respond positively. The interviewee will have a different attitude toward each of the presented concepts. He will have an attitude regarding child abuse, a different attitude toward negligence, again for manslaughter and so on down the line. These attitudes will influence his subsequent behavior. Because attitudes are learned and relatively enduring, the likelihood of the interviewer changing the interviewee's attitude during the interview process is remote. The key is not to try and change the interviewee's attitude, but rather to find a frame that embodies an attitudinal component for which the interviewee has an emotional acceptance.

Application Question

What would be possible frames for a case involving:
- missing money;
- fraud;
- hit and run;
- internal theft?

886 IR: Now, first degree murder carries what? Do you know?

887 IE: No.

Note: The use of a question at this point continues to cause the interviewee to think.

888 IR: That's a life sentence. That's mandatory life. We can go all the way down
889   to negligence which carries a few years. Or even child abuse, misde-
890   meanor child abuse which carries you know it's a misdemeanor term. OK.

891 IE: OK.

892 IR: OK. So it's a very important decision that the DA is going to make. OK.
893   Whatever decision he makes it's going to go onto court. Right? Unless
894   they don't charge you with anything.

895 IE: Right.

896 IR: OK. It's going to go onto court probably and there'll be a case. And
897   eventually that case will go before twelve people in a jury.

898 IE: Right.

899 IR: Right. And those twelve people are going to get to see this tape. They
900　　are going to get to see what you said. How that you held the baby and
901　　all those kinds of things.
902 IE: That's, that's totally fine.
903 IR: Right.
904 IE: 'Cause everything that I told you is true.
905 IR: OK.
906 IE: And that's, that's the way it happened.
907 IR: OK. And here's what I want to tell you, Andrew.
908 IE: OK.
909 IR: OK. What you are telling me doesn't add up. And so what they're
910　　going to hear is just that.

Note: At this point the interview has transitioned into the Red Zone. To a greater or lesser degree the interviewer has expressed his disbelief in the presentation of the interviewee. This expression could be implicit or explicit. However, the onus is now upon the shoulders of the interviewer to "make his case" and persuade the interviewee. Within the Red Zone, the interviewer is tasked with moving from an information gathering and confirmation phase to implementing the communication devices that will produce the behavioral outcome which has been planned for all along. This zone is the transitional area between the Green Zone and the Gold Zone.

Coaching Point:
- With line 909 the interviewer has transitioned from the Green Zone into the Red Zone.
- When transitioning into the Red Zone, do not respond emotionally or in kind to the negative comments or behavior of the interviewee. Use their anger. Do not be used by their anger. Listen specifically to what the individual is saying. What topic does the individual utilize to express his anger? Is the individual giving specific denial or has he placed his anger onto some peripheral issue?

911 IE: What do you mean it doesn't add up?
912 IR: I'm going to explain that to you.
913 IE: OK.
914 IR: What I want you to think about is this. If you were one of those twelve

Note: Usage of the word "*think.*"

915   people and somebody else was sitting there in front of you, would you
916   rather hear from them, "Ah, hey, it was an accident. I didn't mean for
917   it to happen this way. I lost my temper. I'm not that kind of a guy. I
918   would never intentionally hurt a child. I might have just got frustrated
919   for a second."

Note: The continual usage of language to activate the interviewee's cognitive process.

Application Question

Why do you think the interviewer is now using the frames:
- accident;
- I didn't mean for it to happen this way;
- I lost my temper;
- I'm not that kind of a guy;
- I would never intentionally hurt a child;
- I might have just got frustrated for a second?

Application Question

What do you think would be the results of the utilization of those frames?

920 IE: No.
921 IR: No. I'm just telling you. I want you to think about it.
922 IE: I don't get frustrated.
923 IR: I want you to think about it.
924 IE: OK.

Application Question

What do you think is the significance of the interviewee's response here of "*OK*"?

Summary

During this section we have examined the concept of persuasion. We note that thinking precedes behavior. Additionally, the roles of values, beliefs, and attitudes were linked to the persuasion process. Lastly, the importance of frames as a vehicle for persuasion was addressed. All of the presented elements are directed towards exercising an emotive effect on the thought process of the interviewee.

Note: Located in Appendix C is a "Persuasive Interview Strategic Plan" form that may serve as a resource as you plan for persuasive interviews that incorporate the information and concepts presented in this text.

Chapter Two

Initiating Cognition in the Interviewee's Mind

A companion's words of persuasion are effective.
Homer (ca. 800–700 BC), *The Iliad*

We will continue our journey with further examination of the next segment of the interview and the persuasion techniques used.

Exercise 1, Chapter 2

Read the following portion of the transcript thoroughly.

925 IR: Because if you don't, if you hear this, what you've told me today.

926 IE: Right.

927 IR: And then all the physical evidence that we have and witness state-
928   ments that we have and the neighbor's statements that we have had
929   come in and they don't support anything that you said, and you were
930   the only person who was alone with that child.

931 IE: Uh, Um.

932 IR: And they're thinking to themselves, "I'll bet he meant for this to hap-
933   pen." I mean, maybe they'll say to themselves, "You know what? This
934   guy wanted to get rid of this kid because he didn't want Ann sharing
935   that kid's attention." If they, if you leave it up to those people to try
936   and decide what you were thinking.

937 IE: OK. I'm listening but now that you have said that. I know that that's
938   something that stems from Ann. 'Cause she always tells me that I'm
939   jealous of her. And I'm like, you know, "What, what do you mean?"

940 IR: So Andrew, what I'm trying to tell you is if this was an accident.

941 IE: It was.

942 IR: And if you didn't intend for this to end up like it did today, you need
943   to say that now. This is your chance. Because I can tell you this. I want
944   to tell you this. I saw the x-rays.

945 IE: OK.

946 IR: I saw the scan. That injury, the child could not have lived two weeks
947   period. And I know, let me tell you this, especially in children, bone
948   grows very fast.

949 IE: Right.

950 IR: Babies heal very fast. If that was a two week old injury.

951 IE: Uh, uh.

952 IR: You would see that. I mean it's as clear as day. There's no doctor in the
953   world that wouldn't get on the stand and testify.

954 IE: But, but there's no way that I mean 'cause I didn't touch the child today
955   other than that. And I swear, I, I put that on everything you know.

956 IR: OK. I'll tell you what the doctors told me today.

957 IE: OK.

958 IR: That baby's head impacted against a hard surface today.

959 IE: Today?

960 IR: Today.

961 IE: There's, there's no way it could have impacted today.

962 IR: Well then Andrew, I guess everybody's going to have to try and sec-
963   ond guess you. If you won't tell us. You won't explain why it happened
964   the way it did.

965 IE: I would explain to you if it happened any other way.

966 IR: I don't think that you will.

967 IE: I swear to God I would. There is no other, there is nothing that I did to
968   that child.

969 IR: Does science lie?

970 IE: I don't know.

971 IR: No.

972 IE: I don't believe it does.

973 IR: No. Because they're facts. The facts are going to show that that injury
974   occurred today.

975 IE: But, how could that injury have occurred today?

976 IR: That's what I want to know. I wasn't there. You were the only one there
977   based on your own statement.

978 IE: There is no way that that injury occurred today.

979 IR: Andrew, we have neighbors who hear some stuff going on over there.
980   I tell you.

981 IE: They probably heard me panicking to death calling 911.

982 IR: I want you to know that you have a chance here to explain things. And
983   maybe have it come out a lot different than first degree murder. Maybe
984   you have an anger management problem. Maybe you just need some
985   counseling when it comes to dealing with kids. Maybe you're a pro-
986   bationary kind of person. You know, you got a good job. You got a nice
987   house. You take care of things. If this wasn't intentional, I mean I don't
988   think you picked this baby up and threw it against the wall.

989 IE: I, I didn't pick the baby up and throw it against the wall.

990 IR: But Andrew.

991 IE: I don't know.

992 IR: There's no reason not to tell these people the truth so that they can un-
993   derstand what was going through your mind. Don't make people guess.

994 IE: OK. I, I was just trying, trying to think of any reason that it is.

995 IR: OK. I've had some cases before where people get a little frustrated.
996   I've been around a lot of babies. They cry. They get on your nerves.
997   They bug you. You get tired of it. You think, "I shouldn't be taking care
998   of this baby. This isn't my baby. This isn't my job." Maybe some peo-
999   ple shake it like this and put it down. They don't intend to cause any
1000   injury to the child. They didn't mean for anything to happen to the
1001   baby. Maybe they put the baby down hard in the crib and while they
1002   did that the baby's head strikes the edge of the crib. Things like that
1003   happen. That happens to people.

Breakdown—Analysis of the Transcript and the Persuasion Process Segment Two

Now that the second segment of the transcript has been read, we will systematically examine the persuasion dynamics encountered in this section.

925 IR: Because if you don't, if you hear this, what you've told me today.

926 IE: Right.

Note: In line 925, the interviewer is using the term *"because,"* which is an explainer, or a term used "to give the reason for or cause of."[8] The interviewer is explaining to the interviewee the importance and magnitude of his response on his future destiny and freedom. The interviewer is attempting to make the subject realize that his previous responses were unbelievable to a jury and therefore unacceptable to the interviewer. By forcing the interviewee to initiate the cognitive process of explaining how the jury is likely to perceive his answers, the interviewer has made him think about the consequences of his answers.

Coaching Point

- Give a rationale whenever you are articulating a consequence. You can emphasize the positive aspect of cooperation or the negative aspect of non-cooperation. However, doing both can make your assertion synergistic.

927 IR: And then all the physical evidence that we have and witness state-

928   ments that we have and the neighbor's statements that we have had

929   come in and they don't support anything that you said, and you were

930   the only person who was alone with that child.

931 IE: Uh, Um.

Note: Between lines 927 and 931, the interviewer has listed all the supporting evidence in his possession that refutes the statement of the interviewee:

- the physical evidence;
- witness statements;
- neighbor's statements.

By presenting these collectively, the interviewer has strengthened his assertion that the interviewee's account of the evening is fictitious. The interviewee may be able to successfully deny, ignore, or overcome with his defense each of the items listed by the interviewer when they are presented individually; however, when presented collectively, they present a demoralizing front the interviewee cannot overcome. The strength of the interviewer's presentation is in the number of items presented at once, as opposed to presenting them one at a time. In line 929, the interviewer states none of the evidence supports *"anything that you said."* The result in the mind of the suspect is the realization he is fighting an uphill battle against multiple adversaries. If the facts had been presented individually, the interviewee may have felt more confident in his ability to refute or deny one element and possibly two, but not a successive list of multiple items that, when presented as a whole, indicate his story was fabricated. The beauty of this tactic is the presentation of all the items together as opposed to individually; this weakens the interviewee mentally and compels him to realize the extremity of the situation he is in and the strength of his opposition.

Coaching Point

- Endeavor to present a minimum of three refuting elements simultaneously.

932 IR: And they're thinking to themselves, "I'll bet he meant for this to hap-
933   pen." I mean, maybe they'll say to themselves, "You know what? This
934   guy wanted to get rid of this kid because he didn't want Ann sharing
935   that kid's attention." If they, if you leave it up to those people to try
936   and decide what you were thinking.

Note: The interviewer has followed up his inventory of the facts of the case and initiated cognition on the part of the subject by confronting him with the conclusions jury members will most likely reach when they are presented with those facts. The interviewer has laid this out in such a manner that the interviewee accepts and believes the image because, if the situation was reversed and the subject was a jury member himself, he would be having the same thoughts, doubts, and questions regarding the veracity of the statements.

937 IE: OK. I'm listening but now that you have said that. I know that that's
938   something that stems from Ann. 'Cause she always tells me that I'm
939   jealous of her. And I'm like, you know, "What, what do you mean?"

Note: These three short lines convey a great wealth of information from the interviewee regarding his willingness to be persuaded as a result of the interviewer's previous strategies. The interviewee confirms that the strategy of making him realize the weakness of his defense in the jury's eyes has been successful. This is evidenced by examining the statement in detail in lines 937–939. The initial indication appears to show a willingness to being persuaded to confess by the argument he is confronting, *"OK. I'm listening."* However, after examining what he is truly saying it is apparent this determination is false. The use of the abjuration term *"but"* appears. An abjuration term is one which "serves to withdraw the assertion made in the previous clause of the sentence."[9] In short, Andrew is saying, "Even though I am telling you I am listening, I really am not." Once the interviewee realizes that he will appear defenseless in the eyes of the jury, he attempts to shift the blame onto Ann with an explanatory sentence: *"'Cause she always tells me that I'm jealous of her."* He is challenging the idea of his being jealous of the child as a possible motive. In the end a second person reference is used *"And I'm like, you know,"* which "diverts attention from himself"[10] and "signals that he feels no personal accountability or responsibility for what has happened."[11]

Coaching Point

- Attend to the verbal, vocal, and non-verbal behavior of the interviewee in order to become cognizant of the accountability shifts. If the accountability shifts with your persuasion objective then adjust accordingly. If not, then use questions to reinforce your presentation.

940 IR: So Andrew, what I'm trying to tell you is if this was an accident.

941 IE: It was.

Note: The frame "accident."

Note: The interviewer has utilized the frame of an accident to gauge the receptiveness of the subject to that avenue of persuasion. The interviewee's emphatic affirmative response of *"It was,"* indicates his receptiveness to the idea of the incident being framed as an accident. An interview strategy should be developed to explore the avenue of persuading the subject to confess by presenting the incident in the form of an accident. The interviewee's positive response to the frame and his seizing of the opportunity to explain the incident as an accident indicate his hope of convincing the interviewer of such and his hope that the issue will be left at that.

Application Question: What other frames could the interviewer have considered?

942 IR: And if you didn't intend for this to end up like it did today, you need
943   to say that now. This is your chance. Because I can tell you this. I want
944   to tell you this. I saw the x-rays.

Note: The interviewer has worded his statements utilizing the following frames:

- accident;
- immediacy or urgency to confess now;
- his only opportunity or chance to confess;
- the investigator's knowledge of what really happened;
- collectiveness.

The interviewer has perceptively identified the openness of the subject to be persuaded to confess by using the avenue of describing the incident as an accident. This is reiterated in his statement. By using this mechanism, he provides the interviewee an opportunity to confess, and he increases the psychological pain and stress felt by the interviewee by emphasizing the need for immediacy in the confession, as seen in the following statements: *"you need to say that **now**"* and *"this is your chance."* The use of these statements implies to the interviewee that "If you confess now, the psychological pain and stress experienced will be less severe than waiting,"—a mental amnesty if you will. The interviewer is also attempting to reach out to the interviewee as someone who has the interviewee's best interest at heart, a collectiveness implying they are in this together, by stating, *"I want to tell you this."* In the mind of the interviewee, the use of this phrase is interpreted as a show of concern by the interviewer. The interviewer's first statement *"because I **can** tell you this"* comes across as strictly by the book and very impersonal. He is telling me this because he can, because he is allowed to. In contrast, the second statement, *"I **want** to tell you this,"* implies a personal bond between the interviewer and interviewee—"He is telling me this because he wants to." In society, the verb **can** is used to describe acts that we **have to do** as a result of the demands of our careers or personal lives. I can take out the trash, I can pay my bills, I can write an incident report. The verb **want**, however, is used to describe acts that we desire to accomplish of our own free will—our completion of them is optional. I want to go on vacation, I want to win the lottery, I want to help the people in my life that I care about. By using the verb **want** the interviewer has made the interviewee feel as if there is a personal bond between them, a collectiveness indicating the interviewer and subject are in this together, and the interviewer cares about the best interest of the interviewee.

Coaching Point

- Never underestimate the power of "connecting" with the interviewee. Toward that end, do not take the case or the actions of the interviewee personally. Doing so will only negatively effect your ability to influence the behavior of the interviewee.

Application Questions

1. Are there particular cases that are especially troublesome to you?
2. How do these negative feelings impact your effectiveness as a persuader?
3. What do you need to do to reduce or eliminate your own emotional response?

945   IE: OK.

946   IR: I saw the scan. That injury, the child could not have lived two weeks

947   period. And I know, let me tell you this, especially in children, bone

948   grows very fast.

949   IE: Right.

Note: The following frame was used in this statement by the interviewer:

- facts;
- medical evidence.

The interviewer has interjected a factual observation, *"I saw the scan. That injury, the child could not have lived two weeks period,"* that includes known medical evidence. His revelation that he has actually viewed the scan himself removes in the interviewee's mind his opportunity to argue that the injury was not severe or life threatening. The interviewer further states a medical fact that the interviewee knows to be true: *"and I know, ... especially in children, bones grow very fast."* The interviewee knows the veracity of this statement and has to agree with it. This successfully excludes any debate about when the injury actually occurred.

Coaching Point

- Present your refuting arguments in a timely and appropriate manner. Do not react negatively to any possible adverse reactions of the interviewee to your presentation. Pay close attention to what the interviewee is saying during the times of loss of self control. This can be a time when the interviewee is most vulnerable and most likely to reveal him-

self. By answering anger with anger, the only result is that now there are two weak individuals that are out of control.

950 IR: Babies heal very fast. If that was a two week old injury.

951 IE: Uh, uh.

952 IR: You would see that. I mean it's as clear as day. There's no doctor in the

953   world that wouldn't get on the stand and testify.

Note: Continuing with the frames of factual presentation of the medical evidence that he has previously used, the interviewer removes any possible credibility of the interviewee's defense that the injury occurred two weeks earlier by stating *"Babies heal very fast; if that was a two week old injury."* This assertion implies that an injury that occurred in that timeframe would show up on the scan as unmistakably different than an injury that had occurred more recently would. *"You would see that."* He furthers this with *"it's as clear as day,"* thus removing any hope that any possible doubt as to when the injury occurred exists. The interviewee's hope of finding someone who would defend and support his version of the story was further reduced by the statement *"There's no doctor in the world that wouldn't get on the stand and testify."* This also reinforces the following thought pattern of the interviewee: he is alone in his attempt to defend himself by stating that the injury occurred two weeks previously, and no one is going to believe his version of when the injury occurred. The presentation of overwhelming evidence and the opinion of medical professionals in direct contradiction to his statement further reduces his chances of presenting a believable defense in the eyes of the jury. In other words, there is no one willing to help him and he is alone in his belief of his version of the events as plausible.

954 IE: But, but there's no way that I mean 'cause I didn't touch the child today

955   other than that. And I swear, I, I put that on everything you know.

Note: Several issues are apparent in this response. First, the use of an abjuration term or retractor in the beginning of the sentence indicates his negating the previous statement made by the interviewer. The use of the word *'cause* explains or supports his denial. *"There's no way ... 'cause I didn't touch the child today other than that."* Let's look at this statement in depth. The paramount issue to observe in this statement may not be what the person has said, but instead what he has chosen not to say. He is not saying, "I did not touch the child," which is what we would expect an innocent person to say. Instead he emphasizes and says, "I did not touch the child **today**." The other interesting component of this statement is the phrase *"other than that,"* which is being used as an equivocating term, "allowing the speaker to evade the risk of commitment,"[12] in this case of the specific touch that resulted in the fatal injury. Andrew is not saying he absolutely did not touch the child, but instead he is saying, "I didn't touch the child *'other than that,'*" which indicates that the child was in fact touched by him in some manner. The use of *"I swear"* is viewed as a weakened assertion that is "indicative of the speaker's need for additional support for what he has said."[13] And finally, second person collective referencing is displayed in the statement *"you know,"* indicating the speaker's attempt to include the listener as an integral part of what is occurring and diverting attention from himself.

Coaching Point

- Attend to every word the interviewee is saying. Every word is important. The frame which will be most conducive to influencing his behavior will often be found within the terms the interviewee uses to express himself. At the very least, as he articulates, he is providing some insight into his world, his frames, and his attitudes. Listen, learn and respond.

956 IR: OK. I'll tell you what the doctors told me today.

957 IE: OK.

958 IR: That baby's head impacted against a hard surface today.

959 IE: Today?

960 IR: Today.

961 IE: There's, there's no way it could have impacted today.

Note: In lines 956–961 the interviewer has framed his statement around the timeframe and is focused on when the injury occurred. His presentation is based on the medical determination of when the injury was sustained. The interviewee feigns surprise at the fact of when the injury occurred. The interesting component in this is that the interviewee is not surprised that an impact has occurred at all, but at the fact the injury has occurred today.

962 IR: Well then Andrew, I guess everybody's going to have to try and sec-
963   ond guess you. If you won't tell us. You won't explain why it happened
964   the way it did.

965 IE: I would explain to you if it happened any other way.

966 IR: I don't think that you will.

967 IE: I swear to God I would. There is no other, there is nothing that I did to

968   that child.

Note: The frames used in this interchange are:

- the interviewee's opinion versus everyone else's opinions;
- reluctance to provide an explanation.

The interviewer has increased the psychological stress on the subject by emphasizing the fact no one will believe his version of the events. The result of this will be that the jury will form their own conclusions as to how the child was injured, which may be more disastrous to Andrew than his just admitting the truth. In line 965, Andrew is not denying that the injury occurred or his responsibility for the injury, instead he is stating *"I would explain to you if it happened **any** other way."* The operative word in this statement is any. There is no emphatic denial of the impact but instead a denial of how it happened. Andrew uses the weakened assertion of *"I swear to God"* in an attempt to support his belief in his version of the facts. In the last sentence Andrew catches himself making a mistake in his statement of denial. He begins with the phrase, *"There is no other"* then adds to it the following, *"there is nothing that I did to that child."* As he is speaking this sentence, Andrew realizes he has provided the interviewer a sign, a "linguistic unit that is the symbol of an idea,"[14] and as a result he has opened a potential area of vulnerability for the interviewer to exploit. When he makes the statement *"there is no other,"* he implies he did do *something*, just not what was being referred to at the moment. Denial or negation is used to allow the speaker to *"disavow or deny thoughts, feelings, wishes or needs that cause anxiety."*[15] He is not initially stating *"that there is nothing that I did to that child"* as an innocent person would normally do; instead his sentence starts with *"there is no other,"* which he realizes conveys that he did do something to the child, just not what he was being questioned about. His resulting action is to stop mid-sentence and interject the more expected thought of *"there is nothing that I did."*

Application Question: In what other manner might the interviewer have induced psychological stress?

969 IR: Does science lie?

970 IE: I don't know.

971   IR: No.

972   IE: I don't believe it does.

973   IR: No. Because they're facts. The facts are going to show that that injury
974   occurred today.

975   IE: But, how could that injury have occurred today?

976   IR: That's what I want to know. I wasn't there. You were the only one there
977   based on your own statement.

978   IE: There is no way that that injury occurred today.

Note: The following frame is evidenced in this interchange:

- scientific facts.

The interviewer is asserting the validity of medical and scientific facts to the interviewee. His goal is to get the interviewee to accept in his mind the factual basis of the scientific and medical evidence that establishes the injury occurred today. Ultimately, the goal is to persuade the interviewee to admit to causing the injury, based on the evidence presented, by essentially making him realize that his denial contradicts the scientific and medical evidence. Andrew is emphatic in his statement *"there is no way that that injury occurred today."* It is interesting he doesn't say that no injuries occurred today or at any other time, but simply *"that that injury occurred today."*

979   IR: Andrew, we have neighbors who hear some stuff going on over there.
980   I tell you.

981   IE: They probably heard me panicking to death calling 911.

982   IR: I want you to know that you have a chance here to explain things. And
983   maybe have it come out a lot different than first degree murder. Maybe
984   you have an anger management problem. Maybe you just need some
985   counseling when it comes to dealing with kids. Maybe you're a proba-
986   tionary kind of person. You know, you got a good job. You got a nice
987   house. You take care of things. If this wasn't intentional, I mean I don't
988   think you picked this baby up and threw it against the wall.

989   IE: I, I didn't pick the baby up and throw it against the wall.

Note: The frames utilized are:

- witness statements;
- opportunity to confess;

- anger management;
- compliments;
- accident.

The interviewer begins his discourse by stating *"we have neighbors who hear stuff going on over there."* This immediately plants the question of "what stuff have they heard and relayed to the police" in the interviewee's mind. In response the subject uses *"probably"* to equivocate in his defense. He does not say, "They heard me panicking to death," because that was not what was occurring. Instead he says they *"probably* heard me panicking," which can also be interpreted as they "probably also heard me doing something else."

After this exchange, the interviewer provides various alternatives to the charge of first degree murder to the interviewee, in an attempt to determine if any of those options are viable means of persuading the interviewee to confess. The interviewer is appealing to the interviewee's sense of reasonableness by providing him *"a chance here to explain things."* The interviewer is also providing plausible alternative frames such as: maybe *"you have an anger management problem"* and *"maybe you just need some counseling when it comes to dealing with kids."* The interviewer presents probation as an alternative to a life sentence, to provide hope to the interviewee if he admits the offense—probation may be a possible outcome if a confession is forthcoming. With each of these frames, the interviewer is engaging the interviewee's cognitive process regarding the incident and his options. In lines 985–987, the interviewer describes the positive traits of the interviewee: *"Maybe you're a probationary kind of person. You know, you got a good job. You got a nice house. You take care of things."* These statements compliment some of Andrew's attributes and would be disarming to the interviewee, as we normally do not compliment those who we think negatively of. In positively describing Andrew, the interviewer has mentally disarmed him into believing that maybe he doesn't view him as a "bad guy" and would be willing to help him.

In line 989, the interviewee states: *"I didn't pick the baby up and throw it against the wall."* Two things are apparent in this statement. First is the use of a non-personal reference word *"it"* when referring to the baby. Instead of referring to the baby by her given name, or even as *"the baby,"* as he has throughout the interview, in this case Andrew refers to her by the non-personal term *"it."* Non-personal reference may indicate "an avoidance of intimacy and responsibility."[16] Second, Andrew is very emphatic in his statement of denial, which he hopes will lead to the conclusion that this statement is truthful. The interviewer, however, remains focused on his objectives and explores with Andrew other possible ways in which the baby may have been injured.

Application Question: What effect did the interviewer's use of the word "maybe" have on the power of his presentation of the different frames?

990 IR: But Andrew.

991 IE: I don't know.

992 IR: There's no reason not to tell these people the truth so that they can un-
993   derstand what was going through your mind. Don't make people guess.

994 IE: OK. I, I was just trying, trying to think of any reason that it is.

Note: In lines 990–994, the interviewer is providing Andrew with the opportunity to offer his version of what happened to the jury as a manner of explaining to them the events leading up to and of the actual incident. He is establishing the thought in Andrew's mind that allowing the jury to **guess** about what happened is worse than telling them what really did happen. Andrew's response is to initially stall by stating *"OK I just, I was just trying,"* since he knows exactly what did happen and could recall and reiterate the events of the incident in total clarity if he had been persuaded to at this point. Instead he is just trying to think of something to say that may support and assist him in his denial of guilt.

995 IR: OK. I've had some cases before where people get a little frustrated.
996   I've been around a lot of babies. They cry. They get on your nerves.
997   They bug you. You get tired of it. You think, "I shouldn't be taking care
998   of this baby. This isn't my baby. This isn't my job." Maybe some peo-
999   ple shake it like this and put it down. They don't intend to cause any
1000   injury to the child. They didn't mean for anything to happen to the
1001   baby. Maybe they put the baby down hard in the crib and while they
1002   did that the baby's head strikes the edge of the crib. Things like that
1003   happen. That happens to people.

Note: The interviewer approaches this verbal exchange with the frames of:

- justification;
- acceptable behavior;

- accident;
- explanation.

In lines 995–1003, the interviewer again provides the interviewee with a reasonable explanation of how the incident could have occurred, as well as the possible reasoning and motivation behind such an act. The interviewer is also trying to form a collective association with Andrew by stating his understanding of what may have driven Andrew to react in the manner in which he did. Typically, we tend to be a homogenous society in which we associate with those who share similar values, jobs, likes and dislikes as ourselves. By presenting himself as understanding and revealing that he has had similar experiences and shared some of the same reactions as Andrew regarding being around babies, the interviewer has established himself as someone the interviewee can relate to. The interviewer states, *"I've been around a lot of babies. They cry. They get on your nerves. They bug you. You get tired of it. You think, "I shouldn't be taking care of this baby. This isn't my baby. This isn't my job."* This provides Andrew a common thought process to bond with the interviewer, as well as a possible explanation for shaking the baby. The interviewer puts forth the physical force used by Andrew as a readily believable behavior resulting from the frustrating action of the baby.

The interviewer again explores the avenue of presenting the incident as an accident. *"Maybe some people shake it like this and put it down. They don't intend to cause any injury to the child. They didn't mean for anything to happen to the baby."* In anticipation of Andrew being persuaded to confess the crime as an accident, he also provides a reasonable explanation as to how this sort of accident could occur: *"Maybe they put the baby down hard in the crib and while they did that the baby's head strikes the edge of the crib. Things like that happen; That happens to people."* The interviewer has identified Andrews' receptiveness to the crime being couched as an accident and has presented an explanation illustrating the commonality of accidents that is cognitively acceptable to the jury. In other words, since the members of the jury have experienced accidents in their life, some of which they may regret, they can understand how Andrew could have accidentally injured the baby.

Coaching Point:
- By presenting your elements through the vehicle of cases and examples you have had in the past, you can implicitly make your point to the interviewee. This methodology avoids any type of direct confrontation

and allows the interviewee to process the information and possible outcomes in his own mind.

Summary

In this segment we have observed the interviewer testing various types of persuasion strategies to determine which one may be the most effective in convincing the interviewee to confess. While the formation of an interview strategy prior to conducting the interview is important, of more importance is the ability to identify which persuasion techniques are being successful, which are not, and the ability to adjust accordingly during the interview itself.

Chapter Three

Transitioning Toward the Acquiescence

I have with me two gods, Persuasion and Compulsion.
Themistocles (527 BC–460 BC),
from Plutarch, *Lives*

In this chapter we will see the interviewer's efforts to persuade the suspect to confess utilizing more intensive and specific interview and persuasion strategies.

Exercise 1, Chapter 3

Read the following portion of the transcript thoroughly.

1004 IE: OK.

1005 IR: Babies are very delicate, little things.

1006 IE: They are. They're very delicate.

1007 IR: So little things can make big things happen. I mean you don't have
1008 to throw a kid against the wall to hurt them. Right? But when the
1009 doctors go in there and they say that the injury occurred on Octo-
1010 ber seventeenth.

1011 IE: I just don't see how that injury could have occurred today. I just …

1012 IR: I'm telling you Andrew that injury occurred on October seventeenth.

1013 IE: I'm just, I'm just trying to think back and I don't see.

1014 IR: The injury occurred from an impact on that baby's head into a hard
1015 surface. Did you go like this?

1016 IE: No. I didn't.

1017 IR: Well then show me what happened. Explain it so that these people
1018 will know.

1019 IE: The only, the only thing that happened today is like I said. When I was
1020 running around you know with the 911, trying to call 911. I was look-
1021 ing for the phone.

1022 IR: Um Uh.

1023 IE: OK. And I know when she was kind of you know kind of getting how

1024   would you say, getting kind of limp. I did you know try to brush a lit-

1025   tle bit of water on her, you know in the sink.

1026 IR: Where was that?

1027 IE: In the bathroom, you know.

1028 IR: Show me that. Show me how you did it.

1029 IE: I just you know, I, I had her like this and I reached over to turn on the

1030   faucet you know just try to slap a little bit of water on her, you know.

1031 IR: This was before 911?

1032 IE: This was right, right before.

1033 IR: And did she hit her head then?

1034 IE: I don't know. I know I was kind of panicking.

1035 IR: Do you think she did?

1036 IE: I don't know. I was just, I was so panicking at that point.

1037 IR: Did you drop her?

1038 IE: No. I didn't drop her.

1039 IR: Because this isn't a little hit.

1040 IE: No.

1041 IR: This is a fracture like that.

1042 IE: I didn't drop her. I swear to God I didn't drop her. And I, you know.

1043 IR: Did you throw her?

1044 IE: No. I didn't throw her. I'm not that, I'm not that way. You know, I know

1045   it's not up to you to believe me. But I swear, you know, I'm not, I'm

1046   not that kind of person. You could ask anybody that knows me. I'm

1047   not that type of person, you know. I didn't throw her, you know. I was

1048   just, I was panicking you know because she was just, you know, she

1049   was coughing, you know. And I just, I, I don't know. I'm trying, I'm try-

1050   ing to think back. Everything's happened so fast.

1051 IR: I want to tell you what I think happened.

1052 IE: OK.

1053 IR: And as a guy I can understand this. OK.

1054 IE: OK.

1055 IR: I think you were tired. You had to get up before you wanted to. You
1056   were watching TV. Ann leaves you with the baby. You didn't really
1057   want to watch the baby but whatever. She had to go take care of her
1058   business. OK. So she's in there, the baby's in there. The baby's eating.
1059   And then the baby starts crying, whatever. You go in there and you
1060   put the baby's bottle back in. Fine, the baby's eating. You go back and
1061   watch TV. You just sit down. You just get settled down to watch TV
1062   and the baby starts crying again. And that can be very frustrating. It
1063   can be very frustrating. And you walk in and you go, "What is wrong
1064   with you?" You pick up the baby, OK. Because you don't know what's
1065   wrong with the baby. It's not your baby. OK.
1066 IE: I, I.
1067 IR: Listen to me, because I can understand this. OK.
1068 IE: OK.
1069 IR: And you were a little frustrated and maybe you put the baby down
1070   too hard. Maybe you picked the baby up like this a little bit. And the
1071   baby accidentally hit its head. You put the baby down. And then you
1072   tried to help the baby. Because you weren't intending to go in there
1073   and hurt the baby. That was not on your mind.
1074 IE: I would never hurt a baby intentionally.
1075 IR: But maybe accidentally, Andrew.
1076 IE: Maybe accidentally but I don't, I don't recall.
1077 IR: Andrew. I don't recall doesn't hold up in court. These people want to
1078   know what got you to the point you were at. That's all. I want to un-
1079   derstand. I want to understand the frustration.

Breakdown — Analysis of the Transcript and the Persuasion Process Segment Three

1004 IE: OK.
1005 IR: Babies are very delicate, little things.
1006 IE: They are. They're very delicate.
1007 IR: So little things can make big things happen. I mean you don't have
1008   to throw a kid against the wall to hurt them. Right? But when the

1009   doctors go in there and they say that the injury occurred on Octo-
1010   ber seventeenth.
1011 IE: I just don't see how that injury could have occurred today. I just …
1012 IR: I'm telling you Andrew that injury occurred on October seventeenth.
1013 IE: I'm just, I'm just trying to think back and I don't see.

Note: In this verbal exchange the interviewer has applied the following frames:

- appeal to reasonableness;
- medical evidence.

He has appealed to Andrew's sense of reasonableness by stating how delicate babies are; this is a statement Andrew must agree with based on common sense. Babies being delicate is a commonly accepted fact which is not open to debate. It also provides a frame of reference for the interviewer regarding Andrew and his truthfulness. Andrew's response indicates his ability to affirm in a positive manner when faced with a question where his veracity is not challenged.

The interviewer has provided Andrew with two areas to be explored with the next statement, *"little things can make big things happen,"* and the date of the injury. In the first, the interviewer has attempted to persuade Andrew to confess by providing him an opportunity to explain the incident as a *"little thing,"* however, Andrew chooses not to be persuaded by this tactic. The interviewer also begins to press Andrew regarding the date of the incident and the fact that medical experts can positively prove the injury occurred on October seventeenth. This fact ties down the interviewer in his latitude on the time continuum. Andrew responds to this statement, replying with *"I just don't see how that injury could have occurred. I just…."* The key component in this statement is the realization Andrew is using the visual sense verb *"see"* in phrasing his response. In addition, Andrew uses repression in this interchange. Repression is expressed in *"various situations and emotions that represent danger to the speaker and that would create anxiety if recognized."*[17] Andrew begins to make a continuation or follow-up statement starting with *"I just…."* Unfortunately, in this example the interviewer interrupts Andrew before he finishes his statement, resulting in our never knowing what he might have said.

In line 1013, Andrew's response indicates he is attempting to stall by stating *"I'm just, I'm just."* He is also using a weakened assertion in the form of the word *"trying."* If he was recalling the events as they had occurred he would not need to *"try"* and think back to remember them; he would just state the memories in a chronological order as they occurred. Andrew is also still using the visual sense verb *"see."* Identifying the sensory channel through which Andrew is cognitively processing information is important—it allows the interviewer to communicate more effectively with him, resulting in a more viable avenue of persuasion.

Coaching Point

- Do not expect the interviewee to readily move to the stage of making an admission. Note the symptomatic indicators listed above and use them to assist in getting a "read" on the interviewee.

Application Question

What would generally be the effect upon a persuasive interview if the interviewer were to:

(1) not recognize the symptomatic indicators for what they are, and
(2) react negatively to those indicators?

1014 IR: The injury occurred from an impact on that baby's head into a hard

1015   surface. Did you go like this?

1016 IE: No. I didn't.

1017 IR: Well then show me what happened. Explain it so that these people

1018   will know.

Note: The frames chosen by the interviewer are:

- statement of fact;
- requesting a visual example of what happened for clarification and understanding.

The statement *"The injury occurred from an impact on that baby's head into a hard surface"* removes some of the vagueness surrounding Andrew's version of the events. It is a statement of fact, supported by the medical evidence, that the babies head did, in fact, impact on a hard surface. The type of surface struck has been narrowed to a hard one, and now the effort will be focused on determining what specific hard surface was struck. The follow-up question, *"Did you go like this?"* indicates the perceptiveness of the interviewer in mirroring his communication style to the visual style Andrew is operating in, thereby increasing the probability of Andrew's being receptive to being persuaded to confess. At this point in the interview process, the interviewer has realized the interviewee is sitting in the visual chair and has correctly modified his strategy to reflect this dynamic. The use of visual terms by the interviewer aids in establishing rapport with Andrew, and once rapport is established, cooperation is more probable. The interviewer's use of wording in the same sensory channel as Andrew's creates a common bond with Andrew. The interviewer demonstrates his question, *"did you go like this?"* This provides an action Andrew can view. The interviewer also states *"... show me what happened"*; the use of compatible sensory terms between the interviewer and interviewee creates a subconscious connection between the two.

Coaching Point

- Always pay attention to the sensory language of the interviewee. Endeavor to match the frame of reference of the interviewee with regard to the expressed topic or action.

Application Questions

How might you respond to the following:

- I *saw* the money on the table;
- He *felt* like I was taking something that belonged to him;
- It *sounded* to me like they were just going to talk;
- That loss was a *bitter* pill for me to have to swallow;
- The whole deal *smelled a little fishy* to me.

1019 IE: The only, the only thing that happened today is like I said. When I was
1020   running around you know with the 911, trying to call 911. I was look-
1021   ing for the phone.
1022 IR: Um Uh.
1023 IE: OK. And I know when she was kind of you know kind of getting how
1024   would you say, getting kind of limp. I did you know try to brush a lit-
1025   tle bit of water on her, you know in the sink.
1026 IR: Where was that?
1027 IE: In the bathroom, you know.

Note: In lines 1019–1021, the interviewer has succeeded in getting Andrew to begin going through the steps of the incident with him. Initially, Andrew is equivocating by using the words, *"The only, the only."* His use of the term *"like I said"* indicates a "referencing to a previous statement."[18] Andrew avoids "the stress related to the deception by prefacing what he is going to say by making a reference to what he has already said."[19] It is true he said it before and by the utilization of the phrase *"like I said"* he is minimizing the anxiety. The interviewee is trying to gain support and complicity from the interviewer by using the the direct referencing phrase *"you know"* numerous times. He also ends line 1021 with an out-of-sequence sentence by stating, *"I was looking for the phone,"* after indicating he was already on the phone with 911 in the prior sentence. Andrew uses a hesitation form in the word *"OK"* in line 1023, however, the more significant component of this sentence is his struggle to recite his version of exactly how the injury occurred. Andrew is gingerly wading into the beginning of recounting the events with his statement of *"And I know she was kind of you know kind of getting how would you say, getting kind of limp."* The use of the false supportive *"kind of"* indicates a *"lack of confidence in his own credibility."*[20] Andrew's use of direct referencing in his statement, *"I did you know try to brush a little bit of water on her"* indicates his *"having difficulty talking and wishes to divert the listener's attention from what he is struggling to say."* Finally, Andrew ends this section with another direct reference of *"you know."*

1028   IR: Show me that. Show me how you did it.

1029   IE: I just you know, I, I had her like this and I reached over to turn on the
1030   faucet you know just try to slap a little bit of water on her, you know.

Note: Continuing to operate in the visual communication channel with Andrew, the interviewer states: *"Show me what. Show me how you did it."* Andrew is using the term *"you know"* and is still speaking in the visual sense, demonstrating how he was holding the baby by stating, *"I, I had her like this,"* and *"I reached over to turn on the faucet."* With this description, the reader can visualize the entire incident. An interesting component occurs in line 1030 where the interviewee states he was just trying *"to **slap** a little bit of water on her."* "Slap" is an interesting choice of descriptive terms to describe what he was doing, since we normally don't slap the people whom we care about or are concerned for. The use of the word "slap" generally is reserved for an act occurring to those whom we do not care about.

1031   IR: This was before 911?

1032   IE: This was right, right before.

1033   IR: And did she hit her head then?

1034   IE: I don't know. I know I was kind of panicking.

1035 IR: Do you think she did?

1036 IE: I don't know. I was just, I was so panicking at that point.

Note: The interviewer has framed this exchange in a:

- chronological order;
- questioning format.

In line 1031, the interviewer asks Andrew a question and Andrew replies, *"This was right, right before."* Notice the word *"right"* is used twice which may indicate stalling on the part of Andrew. The interviewer then asks, in line 1033, *"And did she hit her head then?"* It is interesting to note in Andrew's response that he uses repression in the form of *"I don't know,"* but never explicitly denies the baby hitting her head. "I don't know" is a phrase used when one is unsure of something. In other words, Andrew is stating that he is unsure if she hit her head then. You would surmise that if you were holding an infant in your arms and she struck her head on a sink as a result of your actions, you would know it had happened.

Application Question

What questions would you ask to solidify the fact that the interviewee knew what happened?

1037 IR: Did you drop her?

1038 IE: No. I didn't drop her.

Note: Contrast lines 1037–1038 with the interviewee's previous responses when asked if he dropped her. His response is now *"No. I didn't drop her."* This is a very emphatic denial to the question. The interviewee does not reply: "I don't know if I dropped her or not," instead his response is *"No. I didn't drop her."* This should cue the interviewer to probe for another possible manner in which injury could have occurred; that is, Andrew's dropping her is not a valid option and did not occur.

Coaching Point

- The more you can employ communication strategies that encourage the interviewee to respond, the easier it will become to distinguish his denials that have a factual basis from his attempts to mislead or deflect attention from the truth.

1039 IR: Because this isn't a little hit.

1040 IE: No.

1041   IR: This is a fracture like that.

1042   IE: I didn't drop her. I swear to God I didn't drop her. And I, you know.

1043   IR: Did you throw her?

1044   IE: No. I didn't throw her. I'm not that, I'm not that way. You know, I know

1045   it's not up to you to believe me. But I swear, you know, I'm not, I'm

1046   not that kind of person. You could ask anybody that knows me. I'm

1047   not that type of person, you know. I didn't throw her, you know. I was

1048   just, I was panicking you know because she was just, you know, she

1049   was coughing, you know. And I just, I, I don't know. I'm trying, I'm try-

1050   ing to think back. Everything's happened so fast.

Note: The interviewer frames his questions with a(n):

- description of the injury;
- amplification of the injury description;
- plausible explanation of how the injury occurred.

In lines 1039–1042, Andrew is still adamant in his denial that he did not drop the victim, using an insistence not seen in other questions specifically referring to how the injury occurred. In lines 1044–1047, Andrew states again that he didn't throw her, and his trying to get the interviewer to not judge him or view him in a negative way with the statement *"I'm not that, I'm not that way"* conveys that the interviewer's opinion of him is important to Andrew.

A pivotal moment occurs in the interview at the point when Andrew states, *"I know it's not up to you to believe me."* This provides the careful observer with the first indication that the interview strategy is being successful. If the interviewee did not view the interviewer as someone who cares about his well being, then we would not see this statement being made. It is important to Andrew that the interviewer could have been the one making the decision regarding his future. The opinions we care about the most in life are from those who mean the most to us. It is important to Andrew that the interviewer views him as a good person. This is evidenced by his comment *"you know, I'm not, I'm not that kind of person. You could ask anybody that knows me. I'm not that type of person."* People typically only have concern for the opinions of those who mean something to or are important to them.

This example is also replete with negatives, which *"may be associated with the coping mechanisms of negation and denial."*[21] In lines 1047–1050, Andrew is trying to step over the hurdle of admitting to the crime by telling what happened and yet not telling. His statements of *"I'm trying, I'm try-*

ing to think back," and *"Everything's happened so fast,"* indicate that he is vacillating between wanting to tell and not being ready to tell. He wants to, but just isn't completely committed to doing so yet.

Coaching Point

- At this point the interviewer can be tempted to "step into" the narrative spotlight and attempt to summarize what the interviewee is attempting to articulate. Don't!

Application Question

What communication actions might you take in order to cause the interviewee to commit at this point?

1051 IR: I want to tell you what I think happened.

1052 IE: OK.

1053 IR: And as a guy I can understand this. OK.

1054 IE: OK.

1055 IR: I think you were tired. You had to get up before you wanted to. You
1056   were watching TV. Ann leaves you with the baby. You didn't really
1057   want to watch the baby but whatever. She had to go take care of her
1058   business. OK. So she's in there, the baby's in there. The baby's eating.
1059   And then the baby starts crying, whatever. You go in there and you
1060   put the baby's bottle back in. Fine, the baby's eating. You go back and
1061   watch TV. You just sit down. You just get settled down to watch TV
1062   and the baby starts crying again. And that can be very frustrating. It
1063   can be very frustrating. And you walk in and you go, "What is wrong
1064   with you?" You pick up the baby, OK. Because you don't know what's
1065   wrong with the baby. It's not your baby. OK.

Note: The following frames of persuasion are used in this section:

- alternative theory of what occurred;
- male bonding;
- presentation of a plausible explanation of the incident.

The interviewer provides Andrew with a sympathetic summary of what he thinks happened. Since the concept was presented in such a way, it makes Andrew's actions appear plausible and understandable to him— it creates a commonality between them. The interviewer also appeals to Andrew by invoking their common gender with *"as a guy I can understand this."* His implication is that women might not understand how a baby incessantly crying would be upsetting, but universally men would. This common bond between them allows Andrew to feel safer and more secure confessing to a person who understands and cares about him.

The interviewer then presents his idea of the events leading up to the child's injury. He makes Andrew's frustration with the situation sound normal and completely understandable. The key point to identify in this version of the events is: the baby is responsible for causing the incident, not Andrew, thereby providing him with an escape. He may have committed the crime, but it was not his fault. He was provoked or driven to it by the baby's crying.

Coaching Point

- Remember, shifting the blame to others—a child, a company, a temptation—does not have to make sense to you. The conduct of the persuasive interview is not *about* you, it is only being conducted *by* you. The only rationale that matters is the interviewee's. Likewise, rationalizing actions do not have to fit your sensibilities. If he had your sensibilities, he probably would not be sitting in front of you in the first place.

1066 IE: I, I.

1067 IR: Listen to me, because I can understand this. OK.

1068 IE: OK.

Note: The interviewer frames this as:

- understanding.

Andrew is still stalling and struggling with confessing his guilt. The interviewer attempts to persuade him to confess by strengthening the bond between them—by stating he understands why the incident occurred.

1069 IR: And you were a little frustrated and maybe you put the baby down
1070   too hard. Maybe you picked the baby up like this a little bit. And the
1071   baby accidentally hit its head. You put the baby down. And then you
1072   tried to help the baby. Because you weren't intending to go in there
1073   and hurt the baby. That was not on your mind.

Note: In this exchange the interviewer has used the following frames:

- frustration;
- accident.

The interviewer has provided Andrew with a couple of options. First, he has provided Andrew with the frustration excuse, which may be an avenue that leads Andrew to confess. Occasionally people do things when they are frustrated or angry otherwise they normally would not do. Secondly, the interviewer has provided Andrew with the opportunity of claiming the incident was an accident. The implication is that Andrew's intent was to never harm the baby.

1074 IE: I would never hurt a baby intentionally.

Note: The key word here is ***intentionally***. Andrew is not saying "I would never hurt a baby," but instead he is saying "I would never hurt a baby intentionally." There is a difference. The use of the word "intentionally" implies its opposite: that he recognizes that he might hurt a baby unintentionally.

Coaching Point
- **Pay acute attention to the qualifiers (in the above, "*intentionally*") the interviewee articulates. Qualifiers indicate that in his world, there are exceptions and atypical situations exist. Attending closely and picking up the qualifiers affords you an opportunity to enter his world.**

1075 IR: But maybe accidentally, Andrew.

1076 IE: Maybe accidentally but I don't, I don't recall.

Note: Although Andrew is hesitant in admitting his role in the incident, and denial is apparent along with repression, he has been persuaded to confess the crime, as long as it is described as an accident.

1077 IR: Andrew. I don't recall doesn't hold up in court. These people want to
1078   know what got you to the point you were at. That's all. I want to un-
1079   derstand. I want to understand the frustration.

Note: The interviewer again reiterates the point of wanting to help and understand what actions resulted in the baby being injured. We never see him being accusatory or aggressive in his interview strategy, but instead he is constantly trying to reassure Andrew he understands and wants to help him.

Summary

This segment of the interview reveals the phase in the interview process where the interviewer is attempting to form a bond with the interviewee. The interviewer has begun using the pronoun "we" instead of "you" when referring to the behavior and actions of the interviewee. This bond will help the formation of a complicity between the two, a temporary connection allowing the interviewee to feel comfortable enough in the presence of the interviewer to "let his guard down" and to trust him enough to share the details of the incident with him.

Chapter Four

Frames Rather than Themes

Persuasion is often more effectual than force.

Aesop (620 BC–560 BC)

The journey continues as the initial interview phases have been completed and we now enter the next phase of the interview and persuasion process.

Exercise 1, Chapter 4

Read the following portion of the transcript thoroughly.

1080 IE: I don't know. I didn't, I wasn't frustrated.

1081 IR: Andrew. I know you were and you know you were. And I can see it.

1082 IE: But, I didn't, I.

1083 IR: I know you didn't mean to do it. But let me explain how you did it so
1084   that they can make a good decision. Don't make people base their
1085   decision on this lie that you told a few minutes ago. You know what
1086   I believe? I believe you did fall with the baby two weeks ago.

1087 IE: I did fall with the baby.

1088 IR: But I don't think the baby's been acting much different. And I don't I
1089   don't think the baby suffered any injury that caused her to die today.
1090   And I don't think you do either.

1091 IE: I believe that the baby did suffer an accident. And I don't, I don't.

1092 IR: And do you believe that the baby got an injury on the back of its head
1093   that caused it to die today?

1094 IE: I don't know.

1095 IR: I'm asking you.

1096 IE: I, I hit my head very hard that day.

1097 IR: Andrew. Let me tell you something. That's not it. She didn't. She didn't.
1098   And I can prove it. And if you want a jury to think, "Oh well. This guy

1099   is just trying to lie his way out of it by saying it was an accident." No.
1100   You know what I would want a jury to do? I would want a jury to
1101   know what I was thinking, what I was feeling and what really hap-
1102   pened. Because maybe it is not first degree murder.
1103 IE: It's not murder because I didn't.
1104 IR: Andrew. Andrew.
1105 IE: I didn't murder, murder the child. Well, I didn't mean, I, the part about
1106   her choking and everything with the blood, that's, that's the truth.
1107 IR: So tell me what else.
1108 IE: That's true. I did, I did get her. And I did kind of shake her.
1109 IR: Show me.
1110 IE: 'Cause you know, she was, she was choking. And I grabbed her
1111   mouth, you know. And, and I did stick my finger in there because she
1112   was choking, you know. And after that's when the blood came out.
1113   And I got her and I was like, "Margaret, Margaret" you know, 'cause
1114   she was, you know, she was just going limp on me already, you know.
1115 IR: OK.
1116 IE: And then.
1117 IR: Andrew. Andrew. Before you go any further. Before you do some-
1118   thing that you don't want to do. OK. There's people that I talk to that
1119   what they need is not prison. They don't need to be locked up with
1120   four thousand other guys in a cage. What they need is help.
1121 IE: OK.
1122 IR: Maybe you're a guy that needs help. But, I've never once see a guy
1123   that needs help that didn't ask for it.
1124 IE: Well, can I get some help?
1125 IR: You have to tell the truth. You have to show me that it was a mistake,
1126   that it was an accident. You have to show me exactly what you did.
1127   It's going to match what we find in the coroner's report tomorrow.
1128   And I can talk to the district attorney about you needing help. If that's
1129   what you need try to show us.
1130 IE: I did. I, I shook her.
1131 IR: Because you were angry.
1132 IE: I was, I was, I was scared.

1133 IR: A guy doesn't need help for being scared.

1134 IE: I was scared though.

1135 IR: But a guy doesn't need help for being scared. A guy needs help for
1136   being angry. Maybe you have an anger management problem.
1137   Maybe you need a little counseling when it comes to parenting. But
1138   you have got to tell me that.

1139 IE: Just, whew. I didn't mean to hurt her at all. But she wouldn't, you
1140   know, she was choking and fidgeting.

1141 IR: That was after, I know.

1142 IE: She did choke too.

1143 IR: I know but that was after. Let's start at the beginning. Tell me the
1144   truth so I can tell the DA the truth. Let's do it right.

1145 IE: OK. I just, after I shook her I put her back in the crib.

Breakdown — Analysis of the Transcript and the Persuasion Process Segment Four

1080 IE: I don't know. I didn't, I wasn't frustrated.

1081 IR: Andrew. I know you were and you know you were. And I can see it.

1082 IE: But, I didn't, I.

Note: The interviewer has framed this exchange using:

- sympathy.

Andrew again uses negation by stating *"I don't know. I didn't, I wasn't frustrated."* In this case Andrew may not have been motivated by frustration but by some other emotional state which has yet to be revealed. Andrew states that he did not know why he reacted the way he did or what happened to the baby. However, Andrew is not denying that he hurt the baby — he denies knowing the reason why he hurt the baby. In line 1081, the interviewer appeals to Andrew's sense of reason again with this statement: *"I know you were and you know you were."* He is attempting to impress upon Andrew that there is no doubt that Andrew committed the offense. Additionally, and rightly so, the interviewer is still referring to things in the visual sense, *"And I can see it."*

Application Questions

(1) Why do you think it is a momentous endeavor for the interviewee to transition toward making an admission?

(2) What consequence of making an admission beyond those imposed by law might be hindering the interviewee from complying?

(3) What language devices should the interviewer utilize in order to identify those psychological barriers in the mind of the interviewee?

1083 IR: I know you didn't mean to do it. But let me explain how you did it so
1084   that they can make a good decision. Don't make people base their
1085   decision on this lie that you told a few minutes ago. You know what
1086   I believe? I believe you did fall with the baby two weeks ago.
1087 IE: I did fall with the baby.

Note: The interviewer has chosen the following frame:

- explanation.

In offering an explanation to Andrew, the interviewer is postulating that the incident was an accident, not an intentional act—"*I know you didn't mean to do it.*" Andrew has accepted this and indicated receptiveness to adopting this explanation at this point. In lines 1084–1085, the interviewer makes the statement "*Don't make people base their decision on this lie that you told a few minutes ago.*" This statement is very important, as it is the first time the interviewer uses the word "*lie*" directed towards the interviewee. The other important facet to note here is that the interviewer is removing himself from the hypothetical audience, in this case a jury, and positioning himself as being supportive and on Andrew's side by pointing out the flaws in Andrew's statements and offering him obviously good advice. The interviewer uses the term *people*, not I. By using the personal pronoun 'I,' instead of including himself with the others, he is separating himself from the collective group and is standing alone with Andrew. The word *people,* used in this sense, is a cold, unfeeling term that indicates the lack of emotional bonds characteristic of a relationship that is not close. However, using the pronoun 'I' symbolizes a personal relationship, bond, or closeness between the two.

Coaching Point

- The more the interviewee feels his hands are on the wheel of his own fate, the more he is likely to respond to the frame related theme presented by the interviewer. Endeavor to match these two seemingly at odds undertakings—have the interviewee move in the direction you desire and allow him to think he is guiding the ship by making the decisions. In reality, he is coming to conclusions that were in your mind from the onset.

1088 IR: But I don't think the baby's been acting much different. And I don't I
1089   don't think the baby suffered any injury that caused her to die today.
1090   And I don't think you do either.
1091 IE: I believe that the baby did suffer an accident. And I don't, I don't.

Note: The interviewer has framed his question by utilizing:

- opinions;
- time of injury;
- question seeking agreement.

In lines 1088–1091, the interviewer has indicated his opinions to Andrew regarding the lack of change in the baby's behavior and doubts on when the injury occurred. He is attempting to gain an affirmative response from Andrew with the statement *"And I don't think you do either."* The interviewer has mitigated the impact of the injury in Andrew's mind in an attempt to persuade him to confess that the injury was merely an accident. He realizes the first step in Andrew's confession to the crime is his admitting the incident was an accident. If he is successful in obtaining Andrew's admission to accidentally injuring the child, the full confession is only one more step away. The interviewer has identified some key traits Andrew has consistently used in his denials and is beginning to mirror those terms in his statement, using them to persuade Andrew to confess. For instance, the interviewer presents his statement framed with a lack of assurance or certainty and the frequent use of negation or repression, such as: "*I don't think the baby's been acting much different.*" He did not say "the baby is **not** acting different," but instead said "I **don't think** the baby is acting **much** different." If he had said the baby was acting significantly different than it always had, Andrew would have denied that. A significant change in behavior would indicate something significant had happened to the baby two weeks ago and Andrew is not willing, at this point, to admit to this fact. The interviewer effectively uses the word **much** in combination with the word **different** to describe a minimal change in the baby's behavior. The converse of this is also true, by focusing on Andrew's willingness to admit a slight change in the baby's behavior, he has achieved the first step in obtaining a full confession, a partial admission identifying a change in the baby's behavior occurred indicating a precipitating event. The usage of the statement *"much different"* and Andrew's acceptance of it indicates the baby was indeed acting differently and Andrew is willing to admit this fact. In line 1091, Andrew finally admits what the interviewer so perceptively realized many lines ago: as long as the incident is described as an accident, Andrew is receptive to admitting it.

Application Question

The interviewer continues to emphasize that the interviewee's fate is in his own hands and that he still has the opportunity to make things come out "much different." What do you think the effect of this language will have on the mind of the interviewee?

1092 IR: And do you believe that the baby got an injury on the back of its head
1093   that caused it to die today?
1094 IE: I don't know.

Note: The interviewer has framed this exchange as a:

- question relating to when the accident occurred.

The interviewer asks Andrew a direct and closed-ended question which could be answered with a simple yes or no response, *"And do you believe that the baby got an injury on the back of its head that caused it to die today?"* However, Andrew chooses to answer with the non-definitive and qualifying answer of *"I don't know."* A person who is responding in a truthful manner would be more inclined to respond in a direct manner in the simplest terms possible: yes or no.

Coaching Point

- **With the question on line 1092, as with most questions, be prepared to wait patiently until the interviewee answers. "Silence" is an excellent asset to the persuader.**

1095 IR: I'm asking you.
1096 IE: I, I hit my head very hard that day.

Note: The interviewer asks an open-ended question, *"I'm asking you,"* to elicit the interviewee's version of the series of events leading up to the incident. Instead of explaining what occurred, Andrew responds with a statement which has nothing to do with the question asked: "*I, I hit my head very hard that day.*" Andrew's use of the words "*that day*" in response to a question regarding something that allegedly occurred today indicates he is attempting to avoid the issues and not directly discuss it with the interviewer. One must ask the question what relevance is the interviewee's response to the question asked or the subject being discussed. Andrew's non-sequential statement "those that are out of place or chronological order in the narrative"[22] indicates in Andrew's mind where the importance of the discussion should be placed.

1097 IR: Andrew. Let me tell you something. That's not it. She didn't. She didn't.
1098   And I can prove it. And if you want a jury to think, "Oh well. This guy
1099   is just trying to lie his way out of it by saying it was an accident." No.
1100   You know what I would want a jury to do? I would want a jury to
1101   know what I was thinking, what I was feeling and what really hap-
1102   pened. Because maybe it is not first degree murder.
1103 IE: It's not murder because I didn't.

Note: The interviewer has chosen the following frames:

* statement;
* confrontation;
* options;
* minimization of the offense.

The interviewer takes a firmer, more aggressive stance with Andrew than we have seen before. His statement, "*Let me tell you something,*" indicates to the interviewee that he is not willing to continue listening to Andrew's version of the events. The interviewer also defeats Andrew's attempt to use an accident as the explanation of the event by confronting him with the statement, "*This guy is just trying to lie his way out of it by saying it was an accident.*" The interviewer provides Andrew with his opinion of what he would do if he faced the same situation: "*You know what I would want I would want a jury to do? I would want a jury to know what I was thinking, what I was feeling, and what really happened. Because maybe it is not first degree murder.*" After this statement is made, Andrew responds by saying, "*It's not murder because I didn't.*" In this scenario, the logical conclusion would be that Andrew believes he did not commit a murder because it was not a premeditated act—his intent was not to murder the baby but instead to just stop the baby from crying.

Coaching Point

- The interviewer has to control his or her own non-verbal behavior. To convey to the interviewee that you believe him, you have to look like you believe him.

1104 IR: Andrew. Andrew.

1105 IE: I didn't murder, murder the child. Well, I didn't mean, I, the part about
1106   her choking and everything with the blood, that's, that's the truth.

Note: Andrew again reiterates and supports the conclusion in his mind that he did not *murder* the child; his intent was only to silence the child. He also provides enough information for us to realize that he is on the verge of confessing the crime with his statement *"the part about her choking and everything with the blood, that's, that's the truth."*

1107 IR: So tell me what else.

Note: The interviewer uses the frame of:

- open-ended question encouraging continuance.

The interviewer perceptively realizes Andrew is on the verge of confessing, and he responds correctly to this by asking the open-ended question, *"So tell me what else"* to encourage continuance in Andrew's response.

1108 IE: That's true. I did, I did get her. And I did kind of shake her.

Note: Andrew's response to the question, *"I did, I did get her,"* indicates a stalling mechanism and an admission to the interviewer's statement involving him in the chain of events that resulted in the injury. Andrew has now placed himself with the baby and confessed to shaking her. *"And I did kind of shake her."* The key words in this statement are *"kind of."* In his mind, Andrew is wading into the confession, he isn't outright stating, "I **shook** the baby," nor is he saying "I **didn't shake** the baby," but he is saying "I **kind of** shook the baby," which in his mind may be very close to "I kind of didn't shake the baby."

1109 IR: Show me.

Note: The interviewer continues to rely on the strategy that has been successful thus far, having Andrew sit in the visual chair—*"Show me."*

1110 IE: 'Cause you know, she was, she was choking. And I grabbed her
1111   mouth, you know. And, and I did stick my finger in there because she

1112   was choking, you know. And after that's when the blood came out.
1113   And I got her and I was like, "Margaret, Margaret" you know, 'cause
1114   she was, you know, she was just going limp on me already, you know.

Note: Andrew seeks complicity and understanding from the interviewer with his multiple use of the direct reference phrase "*you know*." It appears important to him that he perceive the interviewer as someone who understands what happened and is sympathetic to him.

1115 IR: OK.

1116 IE: And then.

1117 IR: Andrew. Andrew. Before you go any further. Before you do some-
1118   thing that you don't want to do. OK. There's people that I talk to that
1119   what they need is not prison. They don't need to be locked up with
1120   four thousand other guys in a cage. What they need is help.

Note: The interviewer has framed his question with:

- providing help.

The interviewer provides some advice to Andrew in the form of "*Before you do something that you don't want to do.*" Typically advice is given from one friend to another, not from someone in an adversarial role. Another interesting component here is the use of the statement, "*There's people that I talk to that what they need is not prison. They don't need to be locked up with four thousand other guys in a cage. What they need is help.*" The interviewer provides an avenue of escape to Andrew by holding out the possible alternative of his getting help—murderers go to prison, people whose frustration leads them to commit accidental injury need help.

1121 IE: OK.

1122 IR: Maybe you're a guy that needs help. But, I've never once see a guy
1123   that needs help that didn't ask for it.

1124 IE: Well, can I get some help?

1125 IR: You have to tell the truth. You have to show me that it was a mistake,
1126   that it was an accident. You have to show me exactly what you did.
1127   It's going to match what we find in the coroner's report tomorrow.
1128   And I can talk to the district attorney about you needing help. If that's
1129   what you need try to show us.

Note: The frames used in this section are:

- providing help;
- need for confession.

The interviewer inches Andrew towards a confession with his statement of, *"Maybe you're a guy that needs help. But, I've never once see a guy that needs help that didn't ask for it."* This statement allows Andrew the opportunity to realize that if he asks for help and continues to assert that the incident was an accident, he might have a chance. The interviewer is still relying strongly on the visual chair that has been effective thus far with Andrew: *"You have to **show** me exactly what you did,"* and *"If that's what you need try to show us."* The interviewer is also reaching out to assist the interviewee by offering *"And I can talk to the district attorney about you needing help."* By offering to assist Andrew, the interviewer has again shown him he cares for him and about what happens to him, thus reinforcing the bond of support, since we tend to only help those we care about or are important to us.

1130 IE: I did. I, I shook her.

1131 IR: Because you were angry.

1132 IE: I was, I was, I was scared.

Note: The frame used is:

- anger.

Andrew admits to shaking the baby with his statement of, *"I did. I, I shook her."* The interviewer responds with his suggestion that Andrew was angry when he shook the baby. Andrew replies by asserting that his actions were the result of being scared, *"I was, I was, I was scared,"* not being angry.

1133 IR: A guy doesn't need help for being scared.

1134 IE: I was scared though.

1135 IR: But a guy doesn't need help for being scared. A guy needs help for

1136   being angry. Maybe you have an anger management problem.

1137   Maybe you need a little counseling when it comes to parenting. But

1138   you have got to tell me that.

Note: The frame used is once again:

- an offer of assistance and help.

In this verbal interchange with the interviewer, Andrew's defense of being scared is dismissed, *"A guy doesn't need help for being scared,"* and replaced with *"A guy needs help for being angry."* The interviewer keeps Andrew on course by firmly pointing out that receiving help will require Andrew to admit that he has an anger management problem and take responsibility for his actions (*"you have got to tell me that"*)—help isn't going to be an option for Andrew if he continues to claim that he acted because he was "scared."

1139 IE: Just, whew. I didn't mean to hurt her at all. But she wouldn't, you
1140   know, she was choking and fidgeting.

Note: Andrew experiences an abreaction, a release of emotional tension, as shown by the statement, *"just, whew."* This indicates he has resigned himself to tell the truth about the events concerning the incident. The sigh is a subconscious response to the relief of knowing he does not have to continue the deception, which is stressful to him. However, he still attempts to avoid being totally honest regarding the incident by focusing on the events after the injury was inflicted, instead of detailing the events in a chronological order, or starting at the moment of injury. His statement of *"she was choking and fidgeting"* indicates that Andrew wants to focus on the events that occurred after the injury rather than the injury itself or the events leading up to it, since that timeframe it is more palatable to him.

1141 IR: That was after, I know.
1142 IE: She did choke too.
1143 IR: I know but that was after. Let's start at the beginning. Tell me the
1144   truth so I can tell the DA the truth. Let's do it right.
1145 IE: OK. I just, after I shook her I put her back in the crib.

Note: The interviewer gently states he realizes Andrew is starting his version of the events after the actual injury has taken place, *"That was after, I know."* Andrew's use of a non-sequential statement and his not wanting to disclose the events leading up to the injury or the actual fatal blow itself in a systematic or chronological order is indicated by his statement of, *"she did choke too."* He does not want to discuss the events prior to the choking, which began after the injury, but instead starts at this point in the time continuum. In line 1143, the interviewer is unrelenting in his assertion that Andrew needs to relate the complete story and not just partial facts. He is encouraging, understanding, and supportive in his plea for Andrew to begin at the beginning of the story instead of the end. *"I* *know but that was after. Let's start at the beginning."* The interviewer also does an important thing at this point when he explains to Andrew **why** he needs the information regarding the incident from him, *"Tell me the truth so I can tell the DA the truth. Let's do it right."* As adults, the reason behind an action is important. Cooperation is gained when a reasonable explanation for why something is needed or must happen is presented. Finally, even though Andrew expresses agreement with the interviewer's suggestion of telling the story and telling it accurately, he is still beginning the story at the end rather than the beginning, *"OK. I just, after I shook her I put her back in the crib."*

Summary

During this phase of the interview, the interviewer has persuaded the interviewee to trust him enough to take the initial steps toward a confession. Although he is still hesitant, the interviewee is slowly wading into an admission of the crime. He is "testing the waters" and gauging how the interviewer will react to his confession. As long as the interviewer continues on the path he is taking and does not become intimidating or threatening to the interviewee, he will receive his reward for the time, patience, and effort he has invested in the interview process—a confession.

Chapter Five

Obtaining the Desired Behavioral Outcome

If what the philosophers say be true, — that all men's actions proceed from one source; that as they assent from a persuasion that a thing is so, and dissent from a persuasion that it is not, and suspend their judgment from a persuasion that it is uncertain, — so likewise they seek a thing from a persuasion that it is for their advantage.

Epictetus (c. 50–138 A.D.)

Now the interviewee has progressed to the point of being able to make an admission. While we will see he is not completely at the totally acquiescent goal line, he is getting ever closer. This portion of the transcript is entering the persuasion Gold Zone. This is the juncture wherein the successful closure is at hand, but not in hand. This is not the time to relax and "count your chips," but rather to keep the momentum going until the point of compliance is reached.

Exercise 1, Chapter 5

Read the following portion of the transcript thoroughly.

1146 IR: Start from the beginning.

1147 IE: OK.

1148 IR: You're on the couch.

1149 IE: Yeah. I'm on the couch and she started crying.

1150 IR: OK.

1151 IE: OK. So I went in there and I just, you know, I, I, I did give her, her bot-
1152   tle. And she just, she just wouldn't stop crying. So I grabbed her and
1153   I and I shook her.

1154 IR: Show me.

1155 IE: I just, you know, I was just like, "Margaret" you know just "Please" you
1156   know "Quit crying."

1157 IR: Show me.

1158 IE: I'm showing you.

1159 IR: You're frustrated.

1160 IE: Yeah. You know.

1161 IR: No. I don't want to be mean Andrew. But this doesn't cause an injury.

1162 IE: OK.

1163 IR: Show me.

1164 IE: OK. I picked her up.

1165 IR: Stand up and show me. She's in the crib.

1166 IE: I just, I picked her up.

1167 IR: OK. This is the crib.

1168 IE: Yeah. I picked her up. And I first, I grabbed her. I said, "Margaret" you
1169   know "What's wrong? Why are you crying?" And she wouldn't quit
1170   crying. And it just out, out and I'm like, "Margaret, Margaret. Please,
1171   please quit crying" you know "Please." I didn't know what to do, you
1172   know. Just, "Please quit crying" you know. And I grabbed her head.

1173 IR: Did you really hold the back of her head?

1174 IE: Yeah.

1175 IR: Did you shake her?

1176 IE: I shook her. I shook her. I shook her hard.

1177 IR: Show me because you are frustrated.

1178 IE: I'm showing you. I shook her hard.

1179 IR: That might cause an injury.

1180 IE: I didn't, I didn't mean to though.

1181 IR: Then what happened?

1182 IE: And then I got her and I said, "I'm so sorry Margaret."

1183 IR: No. How did her head get hurt then?

1184 IE: That I don't know.

1185 IR: No. Andrew. You're going back.

1186 IE: OK. When I was shaking her, I hit her back of the head on the crib.

1187 IR: Show me.

1188 IE: You know. Because the crib is up here like this and I was shaking her.

1189 IR: So make that the back of the crib.

1190 IE: Can I make this the back of the crib?

1191 IR: Sure.

1192 IE: And I was shaking her and hit like that.

1193 IR: OK.

1194 IE: And I was like, "Oh. Shit."

1195 IR: And then what?

1196 IE: I just kind of freaked out.

1197 IR: Right

1198 IE: And I was like, "I'm sorry Margaret. I'm sorry." And I laid her back down.

1199 IR: Show me.

1200 IE: You know. I laid her back down.

1201 IR: And then after?

1202 IE: She just started crying harder and she started choking.

1203 IR: Different? Was she crying different?

1204 IE: Just harder. And then she started gasping.

1205 IR: Right then?

1206 IE: Yeah.

1207 IR: What did you do?

1208 IE: I, I you know, I just I kind of lifted her mouth. I was like, "Oh no. What
1209   did I do?" You know, just you know I didn't know. You know so that's
1210   when I did do that finger sweep thing. And then that's when she
1211   started, she started with the blood.

1212 IR: Right.

1213 IE: I feel so bad.

1214 IR: I know you do.

1215 IE: I don't want people to hate me though. 'Cause I'm not that way.

1216 IR: You just made a mistake.

1217 IE: I made a fucking terrible mistake.

1218 IR: You were frustrated, tired of the screaming.

1219 IE: I was just so tired 'cause she wouldn't stop. I didn't mean to do it. The
1220   hitting her head on the crib when I was shaking her, that, that was a
1221   total accident.

1222 IR: Yeah.

1223 IE: I swear to God. I don't want people to hate me.

1224 IR: You didn't go in there intending to hurt her.

1225 IE: No. I didn't, I wouldn't I would never hurt her.

1226 IR: You were frustrated.

1227 IE: Yeah. The thing I told you about the falling, that's, that's the honest
1228   truth.

1229 IR: I believe you.

Breakdown — Analysis of the Transcript and the Persuasion Process Segment Five

1146 IR: Start from the beginning.

Coaching Point

- Once the interviewee has transitioned to this point, have the interviewee revert to the past — the beginning as they have defined it. This movement will help to cement his admission and place all of the events and dynamics into context.

Application Question: What type of questions do you think would be most conducive to having the interviewee return to the beginning?

1147 IE: OK.

1148 IR: You're on the couch.

1149 IE: Yeah. I'm on the couch and she started crying.

1150 IR: OK.

1151 IE: OK. So I went in there and I just, you know, I, I, I did give her, her bot-
1152   tle. And she just, she just wouldn't stop crying. So I grabbed her and
1153   I and I shook her.

1154 IR: Show me.

1155 IE: I just, you know, I was just like, "Margaret" you know just "Please" you
1156   know"Quit crying."

1157 IR: Show me.

1158 IE: I'm showing you.

1159 IR: You're frustrated.

Note: The application of the frame of "frustrated."

1160 IE: Yeah. You know.

Note: The interviewee's acknowledgement—his buying into the frame.

1161 IR: No. I don't want to be mean Andrew. But this doesn't cause an injury.

1162 IE: OK.

1163 IR: Show me.

Coaching Point

- At this juncture, having the interviewee demonstrate and articulate will make his admission physical as well as verbal. This action helps to minimize the possibility of the interviewee recanting his admission at a later time. When you are dealing with a circumstance that did not involve much in the way of physical action, e.g., white collar crime, have the interviewee describe details of the surroundings of the actions—office settings, developing the documents, opening the account, etc.

1164 IE: OK. I picked her up.

1165 IR: Stand up and show me. She's in the crib.

1166 IE: I just, I picked her up.

1167 IR: OK. This is the crib.

1168 IE: Yeah. I picked her up. And I first, I grabbed her. I said, "Margaret" you
1169 know "What's wrong? Why are you crying?" And she wouldn't quit
1170 crying. And it just out, out and I'm like, "Margaret, Margaret. Please,
1171 please quit crying" you know "Please." I didn't know what to do, you
1172 know. Just, "Please quit crying" you know. And I grabbed her head.

1173 IR: Did you really hold the back of her head?

1174 IE: Yeah.

1175 IR: Did you shake her?

Coaching Point

- The use of closed questions to confirm details and circumstance at this point will result in the interviewee committing to his own narrative and is most appropriate.

1176 IE: I shook her. I shook her. I shook her hard.

1177 IR: Show me because you are frustrated.

1178 IE: I'm showing you. I shook her hard.

1179 IR: That might cause an injury.

Coaching Point

- When the interviewee moves, once more, in the directions that are conducive to the ultimate goal, continue to give positive feedback and reinforcement.

1180 IE: I didn't, I didn't mean to though.

1181 IR: Then what happened?

1182 IE: And then I got her and I said, "I'm so sorry Margaret."

1183 IR: No. How did her head get hurt then?

1184 IE: That I don't know.

Note: This is the interviewee's last resistant effort.

1185 IR: No. Andrew. You're going back.

Coaching Point

- Do not be reluctant to address the interviewee's *"going back."* It is not necessary for you to respond in an angry fashion, as if this were an affront to you. You can be firm and in control of your own emotions at the same time.

1186 IE: OK. When I was shaking her, I hit her back of the head on the crib.

Note: This is the point wherein the interviewee has passed into the Gold Zone. The critical admission has been made. In the Gold Zone the interviewer moves into the detail gathering and admission consolidation portion of the interview.

1187 IR: Show me.

Coaching Point

- At this point, explore all of the details of the occurrence minutely. Have the interviewee provide details that only he should know. Explore his feelings and motivations and critical points with regard to what happened. Ask for details about the details. Protect your gains by having the interviewee provide information. Should he recant his admission, the exploratory facts and subsequent confirmations will speak for themselves in defense of the admission.

1188 IE: You know. Because the crib is up here like this and I was shaking her.

1189 IR: So make that the back of the crib.

1190 IE: Can I make this the back of the crib?

1191 IR: Sure.

1192 IE: And I was shaking her and hit like that.

1193 IR: OK.

1194 IE: And I was like, "Oh. Shit."

1195 IR: And then what?

1196 IE: I just kind of freaked out.

1197 IR: Right

1198 IE: And I was like, "I'm sorry Margaret. I'm sorry." And I laid her back down.

1199 IR: Show me.

1200 IE: You know. I laid her back down.

1201 IR: And then after?

1202 IE: She just started crying harder and she started choking.

1203 IR: Different? Was she crying different?

1204 IE: Just harder. And then she started gasping.

1205 IR: Right then?

1206 IE: Yeah.

1207 IR: What did you do?

1208 IE: I, I you know, I just I kind of lifted her mouth. I was like, "Oh no. What
1209   did I do?" You know, just you know I didn't know. You know so that's
1210   when I did do that finger sweep thing. And then that's when she
1211   started, she started with the blood.

1212 IR: Right.

1213 IE: I feel so bad.

1214 IR: I know you do.

1215 IE: I don't want people to hate me though. 'Cause I'm not that way.

Note: The interviewee is revealing his concern for what those who are important in his life think of him.

Coaching Point

• Make sure you understand who is important to the interviewee.

1216 IR: You just made a mistake.

Note: Here the interviewer presents the frame of a *"mistake."* Those persons important to the interviewee will now come to know he made a mistake. He is not a bad person or someone to be vilified—he made a mistake, as all people do from time to time.

1217 IE: I made a fucking terrible mistake.

Note: Here is the interviewee's acceptance of the frame *"mistake."*

1218 IR: You were frustrated, tired of the screaming.

1219 IE: I was just so tired 'cause she wouldn't stop. I didn't mean to do it. The

1220   hitting her head on the crib when I was shaking her, that, that was a

1221   total accident.

1222 IR: Yeah.

1223 IE: I swear to God. I don't want people to hate me.

1224 IR: You didn't go in there intending to hurt her.

Coaching Point

- Utilize affirmations that support and encourage the interviewee's forward motion. Empathy at this point is most appropriate

1225 IE: No. I didn't, I wouldn't I would never hurt her.

1226 IR: You were frustrated.

Note: Emphasis upon the frame of being "frustrated."

1227 IE: Yeah. The thing I told you about the falling, that's, that's the honest

1228   truth.

1229 IR: I believe you.

Summary

In this section we see the efforts of the interviewer come to fruition. We have observed the interviewee's cognition move incrementally toward the goal. These movements have been facilitated, monitored, and course adjustments have been made in order to bring the interview to its successful conclusion.

Note: A complete transcript of the last eighteen minutes of this interview can be found in Appendix B.

Conclusion

Of those individuals whose quotations opened each chapter—Lincoln, Homer, Themistocles, Aesop and Epictetus—Lincoln summarized it best, "a drop of honey" is more productive than "a gallon of gall." In our study, the honey is represented by placing the emphasis on the search for, and the application of, the most productive frame. The gall is represented by the negative qualities of conducting an interview in a judgmental, accusatory, manner, with the interviewer taking the facts of the case personally. As Lincoln pointed out, having the other come to perceive the interviewer as a "friend," confidant, or someone who understands is never going to make the communication event worse. The interviewer is always asking and answering the question, "What is it that will 'catch his heart'?" and moving to employ the same. And we know for a certainty that our cause is just.

If you are so inclined, share your questions or observations with us. Send them to dwrabon@msn.com or te.chapman@hotmail.com and we will continue our discussion.

Appendix A

The Initial Forty Minutes of the Homicide Interview

Note: It is important you read this portion of the interview transcript carefully. The strategy the interviewer utilizes in the last eighteen minutes will not be meaningful without a thorough understanding of what preceded. Throughout this transcript you will see the abbreviations IR and IE. IR represents statements made or questions asked by the interviewer, IE represents those made by interviewee.

1 IR: Well, let's just start by telling me what's going on. What happened?
2 IE: Ok, uh, well, ok, you know. We got up this morning and, you know,
3 my girlfriend she needed to go and get some money out of the bank
4 for her Mom, I guess. Something had happened and she needed to
5 go to the bank. Uh, so, you know, she said, "I need to hurry" you
6 know. And I said, well, you know, "Leave the baby." You know. So she
7 put the baby down and she was, you know, she was sleeping. So I …
8 I think she was sleeping. And she left, you know. Uh, it had probably
9 been several minutes. Maybe, you know maybe five or six. And the
10 baby started crying. You know, and she, kind of unusual, 'cause she
11 cries but softly like she did. So what I did, you know, I went in, you
12 know, and I gave her, her bottle. You know, she was kind of like, you
13 know, lifted her head up, so I rolled her, you know, more or less on her
14 side and gave her, her bottle. Uh, you know, she, she, you know, she
15 started taking the bottle. She had quiet down a little bit, and uh, you
16 know, so I went back into the room, you know, 'cause I was sitting
17 there eating. You know, just had the TV on. It was early. I was just try-
18 ing to eat my food, you know, 'cause I was hungry. And, it … it didn't
19 seem more than a couple of minutes, I would have to say it was in
20 probably another three minutes. I heard her like choking and gasping
21 and uh, you know, I … it … it just was very unusual 'cause I hadn't

71

22   never heard her do that. So I went in there and she was just kind of
23   kicking and flailing her legs. You know, and I was, you know, I was just
24   like, you know, "What's going on here?" And, you know, she was, she
25   was kind of gasping but more or less through her nose. So I kind of
26   opened, you know, opened her mouth to see what was wrong and
27   some fluid came out. It was, I don't, I don't know that I could say that
28   it was formula 'cause it happened kind of quick it was just, you know,
29   just some kind of fluid. And, you know, you know, she started gasp-
30   ing again. And so I just, you know, I didn't know what to do. You know,
31   I figured she's choking, she kicking and gasping. So, I remembered
32   from the first aid that I have, they say you want to try and clear her
33   throat. So I, you know, stuck my finger in her mouth and uh, you
34   know, try to do like, like what they call finger sweep. I believe that's
35   what they call it. And she kind of gasp again and uh, you know, then
36   it was like, it was blood but it was like a real watery type of blood that
37   came out of her mouth. And you know, I … I immediately, I just, I got
38   very scared. Very panicked. I didn't … I didn't know what was going
39   on. Uh, you know, I … there was a washrag that was in the bathroom.
40   I got that and you know, I wiped, you know, wiped her up. And I did.
41 IR: What color rag was it?
42 IE: It was a white one. Like, no, I can't really say white. Like, it was some
43   color. I want to say like, kind of like a really dull pink one you know.
44   Like, although it was probably pink at one time. Uh, I got that and, you
45   know, and I, I tried to wipe her, you know. Tried to pat her down and
46   all of this, you know, thinking to myself, "Oh God, Ann. Get home. Get
47   home." You know, 'cause I didn't know what was going on. And she
48   did another gasp just really, really weird. Just a really weird gasp and
49   she just, her eyes just, you know, I mean, I'll never forget the look on
50   her face. They just got big, you know, like, I think, you know, it's like a
51   look like help me. You know, I … I … I don't know what to and you
52   know. So I, I grabbed her, you know and I picked her up and at that
53   point, I just said, "I have to …" you know, I didn't know what to do. Ann
54   wasn't coming home so I called 911 at that point.
55 IR: What did you tell them?

56   IE: I told them that, you know, I told them, you know, if they could please
57   send an ambulance because I said, "I have a child here that's choking.
58   She's gasping." You know, and at that point she's just, you know, her
59   eyes just kind of closed, and you know, she was just, you know, right
60   here on my shoulder and she spit up again. You know, on my shirt.
61   And I just was very, very scared, you know, I didn't know what to do. I
62   started telling the 911 guy, that you know, "Please" you know,
63   "Where's your damn ambulance? And he's like, "Sir, where's your ad-
64   dress?" And I said, you know, "It's like where I called you." And he said,
65   "I need to know." And I said, you know, I said, "211 South Acme." Uh,
66   so he had me on line and he asked me if she was breathing. And I said,
67   "She gasping!" You know, "I don't … I don't really know if she's breath-
68   ing. I, I think she is," you know. I said, "I think she's breathing." Uh, you
69   know, so then he just, he asked, I told him, "She's just getting more
70   and more pale. And she's getting limp." And so he asked me if I know
71   how to do, you know the breathing technique. And I said, "I" you
72   know, "slightly do" like, you know, like "never really actually did it." You
73   know, but so I just laid her on the couch and I started doing the breath-
74   ing thing. You know, and uh, you know, I got back on the phone. And,
75   you know, he, uh, you know, he asked me, you know, if she was
76   breathing and I said, "I think so." He told me, "Continue." Uh, and right
77   at that time, that's when the paramedics showed up. You know, and I
78   was just very, very, very scared. You know, I, I was just very frightened.
79   You know, I, I didn't know what was going on. And then, you know,
80   my first, my first reaction was, "Oh God, Ann is going to get here and
81   she is going to see all, you know, 'cause there was that blood that she
82   had spit up on the sheet, you know." So, I got the sheet and I said,
83   "She's going to see the sheet and she's going to think that something
84   is very bad." You know, and I didn't want her to freak out because, you
85   know, she's … she's kinda gets kinda hysterical sometimes. You know,
86   so I went and put that in the washer. And you know, 'cause the para-
87   medics had just took her out. And then Ann comes running in. And
88   you know, she's all …
89   IR: You put the sheets in the washer after the paramedics left?

90 IE: Yeah, just right after, I just, you know, I just didn't want Ann to see
91 everything because all of that, I knew she would just go crazy. You
92 know, I mean, if she had seen everything, you know, I didn't, you
93 know, I didn't exactly know what was going on, you know, with Mar-
94 garet. I thought at that time, you know, maybe I did the finger sweep
95 maybe I scratched her or something inside. I didn't know. And I, you
96 know, I didn't want Ann to get totally upset. Uh, you know, so I, I didn't
97 want her to freak out or anything. And next thing you know, next
98 thing I know, you know, the paramedics there, the, the police officers
99 were near by. And uh, they said they had to take her to the hospital.
100 So I know, Ann's mom. I believe she was there. She took off to the hos-
101 pital. And the police officer there, you know, she didn't want Ann to
102 drive. She was hysterical. You know, so she had us fill out papers and
103 she asked me if I could go. But you know, that wouldn't, I know the
104 baby's father was going to be there, you know. I don't think he really,
105 I've never met him, but I don't think he really cares for me. Being, you
106 know, he didn't care for her and me moving in. So Ann just said, you
107 know, it's probably best that I don't go to the hospital 'cause it would
108 have started a confrontation. You know, so I gave her my cell phone.
109 I said, "Make sure you call me, let me know what's going on." You
110 know, "I'm just really worried." So, you know, I just, I stayed at the
111 house. You know, I got down on my hands and knees and I prayed,
112 you know, just told God, "Please, I don't know what's wrong with Mar-
113 garet" but, you know just, you know, "Protect her, keep her safe." I
114 didn't know what else was going on. You know. And at that point, I
115 just, I just felt really bad. I know before the police officers left, I, you
116 know, I was just, I was very, very, I don't know, I don't know how you
117 say just in a state of like shock, disbelief. Uh, so she gave me the num-
118 ber to victim's assistance. And so I did call them and talk to them. And
119 you know, the guy just told me I need to settle down and everything,
120 you know, I cried to them and I told them, I just told them, "I don't
121 know what's going on." You know, I was just very scared, I felt very
122 bad. I felt that, you know, that, you know, that somehow, you know,
123 when I tried to clear her throat, I had hurt her like that. But, you know,

124   after I settled down, and Ann called, she kept giving me updates and
125   she was saying that she had, she had a fracture on her skull. The baby
126   did. And uh, you know, that there was blood on her brain but it was
127   from a previous thing. And I know approximately, uh two and a half,
128   three weeks ago, like that, I was, uh, you know, I was, I was watching
129   the baby and I had just got done changing her. And uh, and I went to
130   go throw her diaper away. I had her 'cause I was going to put her in
131   the car seat, you know, so we could watch TV. And we, we have a big,
132   black telephone cord, you know, it's very long. Uh, you know. I had
133   seen it but I, you know, I thought I had cleared it but when I, it tan-
134   gled on my foot and I had fell. I thought I had protected the baby 'you
135   know, cause I, I hurt my arm. I've still got some marks right there. You
136   know, I bumped my head really good. But obviously, I must have, you
137   know, it must have hit her head too. And, you know, Ann wanted to
138   take her to the doctor. You know, and I told her, well, you know, I said,
139   you know, "Let's just watch her" 'cause I know, you know, when you've
140   got a concussion, you have to go the hospital. You know, and the baby
141   seemed to be fine and everything. But according to what Ann was
142   telling me that what happened …
143 IR: So you told her not to take the baby to the doctor?
144 IE: No, I didn't tell her not to take her to the doctor. I said, let's, you know,
145   let's watch her, you know, and see what's going on and not let her go
146   to sleep.
147 IR: For three weeks?
148 IE: No, not for three weeks. Well, you know, that, that night, you know.
149   You know, she gave her the bottle and the baby went to sleep.
150 IR: And that was how long ago?
151 IE: That was about two and a half, three weeks ago. I would say, I would
152   say more in the neighborhood of about, probably two and a half
153   weeks, you know.
154 IR: OK.
155 IE: And then, you know, after that, you know, the baby, you know, she,
156   she wasn't acting right. She was crying a lot, you know. Being a real
157   crybaby. You know, and I kept telling Ann, well, you know, "You

158   should probably take her to the doctor." You know, 'cause I know she
159   has respiratory problems as it is. "Oh, her check up's coming up," you
160   know. "Her check up's coming up." I believe she said the nineteenth.
161 IR: So Ann wouldn't take her?
162 IE: No. And I, you know, and I told her, you know. I told her, you know,
163   "You should take her," because I said, you know, "That, that flu going
164   around for the kids." You know, I just, just, I didn't know.
165 IR: Was she sleeping at night?
166 IE: Yeah, but she was like, you know, waking more than usual.
167 IR: Crying a lot?
168 IE: Yeah, crying a lot.
169 IR: Was she still eating?
170 IE: She would eat but I, you know, Ann was just, you know, was now try-
171   ing to give her baby food you know. 'Cause she bought her a lot of
172   jars of baby food.
173 IR: Ann was feeding her baby food?
174 IE: Yeah.
175 IR: How was that going?
176 IE: Uh, she wasn't really liking it too much as far as I could tell.
177 IR: Was she urinating blood or anything like that?
178 IE: Not to my knowledge. I know Ann did tell me today that the other day
179   she had thrown up. And she said, "But I thought it was juice." She
180   goes, "But now thinking about it, it was blood." You know, and I was,
181   you know, I was like, "How come you didn't tell me. If you would have
182   told me that" you know, "I don't think I would even have told you to
183   wait to go." "You know, you know, "She might get sick." You know, I
184   don't want to put myself in that kind of predicament.
185 IR: Well, actually there was an accident that occurred two and a half
186   weeks ago that's unreported that may be the cause of this?
187 IE: Yeah. I, there's I, you know, like you said, I accidentally fell there. You
188   know, as soon as Ann got home I told her. You know, I said, you know,
189   see my arms. I have like marks here.
190 IR: Let's go back to that incident two and a half weeks ago. What time was
191   it? Time of day?

192 IE: Uh. Time of day. Time of day. Time of day. I think it was probably, I'm try-
193   ing to think, trying to think, it was probably, roughly about three or four.
194 IR: In the afternoon?
195 IE: Yeah.
196 IR: And who was in the house?
197 IE: It was just it was myself and her son and the baby.
198 IR: The two year old boy?
199 IE: Yeah. The two year old boy. And he was asleep. You know, and uh, I
200   know Ann had left. She went over to her grandmother's. And she told
201   me, "Can you change Margaret?" You know, "She's pretty messy." And I
202   said, well, you know, I don't really like to change diapers but I said, "Yeah,"
203   you know, "I will." And you know, and, and when we fell it even woke
204   the two year up 'cause I heard him yelling, "Mom, Mom." You know, you
205   know, I kind of picked Margaret up and, you know, I was like, "Oh shit."
206 IR: You dropped her?
207 IE: No, I, I fell with her. You know, I was carrying her over here like this.
208   And when I fell, I, I hit my arm. It just happened so fast. I know I did hit
209   the refrigerator door. And that thing just totally, it caught me on the
210   ankle. And I just, you know, I fell. I thought I had protected her but I
211   guess she must have hit her head too. I, I had a really bump right here.
212 IR: You hit your head too?
213 IE: Oh, yeah.
214 IR: Where did she hit?
215 IE: Well, she was right on my shoulder, you know, and I, she must have
216   went over this way as I said.
217 IR: I don't understand. Why don't you stand up and show me what you
218   mean?
219 IE: OK. Well, what I mean, you know, is I, 'cause I was walking and I had
220   the diaper and then the cord it caught my foot and it was this foot
221   here like that. I kind of leaned this way and I hit the refrigerator door
222   and I fell. I fell this way, you know. And I, I hit my head right here.
223 IR: On the refrigerator?
224 IE: No, on the, on the floor. I hit my arm on the refrigerator.
225 IR: Well, how did you fall that way when the refrigerator is right behind you?

226 IE: No it wasn't behind me. It was on the side. I don't know if you have
227   been to the house, see how it is. And I just, I hit like just the handle of
228   the refrigerator.
229 IR: So you fell into the living room?
230 IE: No, I fell into the kitchen.
231 IR: So you spun around?
232 IE: Yeah. I just hit the refrigerator.
233 IR: So you spun around and fell onto the linoleum floor?
234 IE: Yeah. Fell onto the …
235 IR: Where was the baby when you got to the floor?
236 IE: She was right over here over my shoulder. Like up here a little more,
237   you know, I was.
238 IR: Where were her legs?
239 IE: Her legs? Her, her knees were just about right here.
240 IR: And her head?
241 IE: Her head was right next to me. I just didn't know. I kind of just
242   bounced and I'm like, "Oh my God."
243 IR: So what part of her head hit the floor?
244 IE: I would imagine it would have to be like right in this area here.
245 IR: But if you are holding her like this and you're going backwards it
246   would have to be … ?
247 IE: No. No. I was, I was holding her, I was holding her facing forward.
248 IR: You were holding the baby facing forward but you just said her knees
249   were right here?
250 IE: The back of her knees were right here.
251 IR: OK.
252 IE: You know what I mean. You know, like the back part like right here.
253 IR: I have never seen people hold a baby up on a shoulder like that. How
254   do you do that?
255 IE: I was, I wasn't, I was just carrying her like right here.
256 IR: I've seen them do it this way facing forward. Why was she up here?
257 IE: No, I wasn't carrying her up here. I was just holding her like right here
258   with one arm.
259 IR: But she was down below your shoulders so her head didn't hit?

260 IE: She was right, she was right here. No I had her up here because I was.

261 IR: Well how do you hold her face out?

262 IE: I had her like by her legs right here and I was just kissing her.

263 IR: You were holding her by her legs and her face was out and you were
264   kissing her?

265 IE: Not her, not her total legs but you know like right around this area.

266 IR: I'm just trying to get you to explain because I've never seen that before.

267 IE: That's, that's.

268 IR: So her head was right here looking out?

269 IE: Like more or less like right about here.

270 IR: Right here looking out?

271 IE: Yeah.

272 IR: And you said you were showing me on video right there that you had
273   a diaper in this hand and a baby in this hand?

274 IE: Correct.

275 IR: So you're telling me that you had the baby like this facing out?

276 IE: Yeah, because there was just, I was going, going to throw the diaper.
277   Like I said, throw the diaper, come back, you know, and I had her like
278   this. And then I was going to, you know, switch her over here, put her
279   in the car seat.

280 IR: OK. Hang on one second. I'll be right back. OK?

281 IE: OK.

282 IR: OK. I know this isn't exactly the size of a four-month old but that's
283   pretty close. Why don't you show me again?

284 IE: Do I have?

285 IR: Stand up and show me.

286 IE: OK. See I had the diaper like this. I had her about, you know, some-
287   where like that.

288 IR: OK.

289 IE: OK.

290 IR: Now you hit the refrigerator?

291 IE: Yeah, well the, the cord hit.

292 IR: We'll put the refrigerator right here. There's the refrigerator.

293 IE: It was the very edge of the door that I caught.

294 IR: OK.

295 IE: You know, and like I said, I hit my arm.

296 IR: On the door?

297 IE: On, on, well, on the handle.

298 IR: And that's carpeted out there behind you?

299 IE: Yeah, but I didn't go out there.

300 IR: I just want you to show me, that's all.

301 IE: OK. Like this is the refrigerator.

302 IR: OK.

303 IE: Right, here's the refrigerator.

304 IR: Uh, huh.

305 IE: OK. 'Cause you know, the table's over here. So, I came this way and I
306   hit, it just, it caught my foot. So, I went like that.

307 IR: Right.

308 IE: Boom. You know, I, I remember I hit my thing there. I don't, I don't re-
309   call hurting her hitting her head on anything. It just happened.

310 IR: OK.

311 IE: I spun and I just tripped.

312 IR: You spun. Now where did you fall?

313 IE: I fell just straight like this way. I, I stumbled just a little bit. And I fell
314   and she fell with me. So, I know I.

315 IR: You end up on your back?

316 IE: Yeah, with my head and my head like this and the baby was like this.

317 IR: So by the time you got on the floor—I want you to get on the floor
318   and show me where the baby was.

319 IE: The baby was just—I don't need to get on the floor the baby was just
320   lying right here.

321 IR: No. I need you to so I can see. Show me how you were laying down.

322 IE: No, like I say, I'd like to stop right here.

323 IR: You want to stop the interview?

324 IE: Yeah. Because, I'm trying to show you, just, just.

325 IR: Well, I just want to understand what happened, that's all.

326 IE: OK. When I ended up, OK, the baby, I, 'cause I remember I hit like this.
327   Boom, you know, and I just like got up right away.

328 IR: But you could see the baby right next to you?

329 IE: Well, she was still like right in here. You know, I just, I tried, you know,
330   I tried to protect her as much as I could. But I just.

331 IR: OK.

332 IE: I don't understand.

333 IR: OK. I just want to know.

334 IE: I, I remember I grabbed her. It just, it just happened so fast. I freaked out.
335   I don't know for sure if she was like this or completely like this. You know,
336   I do remember that her leg was like, right, you know, right in my arm.

337 IR: She was kind of bent over your shoulder?

338 IE: Yeah.

339 IR: OK.

340 IE: And I just. I hit my head very, very hard.

341 IR: OK. So what happened after that? That day? You get up and what
342   happened?

343 IE: You know, I got up and I just, it was like, oh, man. You know, I just, I
344   was like, you know, just, it sucks. You know, I just, you know, 'cause
345   Ann had left her in my care. I was like, oh my God, you know. Just, I
346   mean, just like, you know, why does this have to happen to me, you
347   know. And you know. So I got Margaret and you know, she's crying
348   and I'm just like, oh man. You know, just, you know, what's going on?
349   You know, so I just, you know, I just started, you know, just trying to
350   comfort her. And you know, then, of course, her son's in the room
351   screaming, you know, "Mom, Mom" 'cause, I guess he heard when,
352   you know, when I fell 'cause that floor's pretty creaky. And also, you
353   know, I told him, you know, like I went in the room, you know, trying
354   to comfort her, holding her. And I had told Stephen, "Are you OK?"
355   And he's like, "Yeah." And you know, he's like you know, "Where's
356   Mama?" And I told him, you know, "She just went" you know. And
357   he just looks at me and he's like, you know, "Is Margaret hurt?" And I
358   said, "Yeah" I said, you know, "We fell" you know. I said, "Did we wake
359   you up?" And he said, "Yeah." And you know, so just, you know, it
360   just really, really, really, you know, just freaked me out. So then I had
361   just put her in the car seat, you know, and I was just kind of rocking

362   her 'cause I, I was just, you know, waiting for Ann. And I told Ann
363   what had happened.
364   IR: How long did it take her to get home?
365   IE: Um, probably about, after I fell, probably about seven or eight min-
366   utes, you know.
367   IR: So really quick afterwards?
368   IE: Yeah. Pretty quick afterwards.
369   IR: And did you think the baby had hit its head at that time?
370   IE: I didn't really know for sure. I, I did like I said, I.
371   IR: You thought you might have protected her?
372   IE: I thought I might have protected her 'cause I was trying to hold her
373   but, you know, with the way that she was. I knew she had first, you
374   know she had hit something, you know, whether it would be the door
375   because when I, you know, I kind of went like this.
376   IR: Did she bleed?
377   IE: No.
378   IR: Did she have any injuries?
379   IE: No, not that I could see.
380   IR: No bruises?
381   IE: Well, she had, she had like a bruise like right here.
382   IR: On the front of her head?
383   IE: Yeah. Just like right really, really, really light. You know, like I said, from
384   probably, I think she might have grazed the door handle with me.
385   IR: Now you know what, she's four months old, so she can't crawl.
386   IE: Right.
387   IR: Does she, can she sit up by herself?
388   IE: She was, she was in the stages of trying to you know lift her head up.
389   IR: But not sit up?
390   IE: No, she can't.
391   IR: Can she roll over?
392   IE: I've only seen her roll over once and I think that's because she had her
393   hand you know stuck. She accidentally did it. Ann said she was, I don't
394   know.
395   IR: Could she hold her own bottle?

396 IE: Uh, not that I know of.

397 IR: So she had to be held when she's fed?

398 IE: Well no because she had this little dog, I guess, well Ann calls it
399   Bernadette. And she likes to hold onto that before we do anything.
400   We put the bottle on that to brace it up.

401 IR: To kind of prop it?

402 IE: Right.

403 IR: OK. Does she burp on her own?

404 IE: Uh, I don't believe so. I think Ann's always burped her.

405 IR: Have you ever burped her?

406 IE: Yeah.

407 IR: Can you show me how you burp her?

408 IE: Yeah. I would just, I would either hold her like that you know and rub
409   right there. Or sometimes just pat real lightly like that you know. Or I
410   know sometimes you know Ann would tell me if she wasn't going to,
411   you know we would hold her up and lean her over a little bit. Just rub
412   like that.

413 IR: On the lower part of her back?

414 IE: Yeah. She would you know, she would burp. That would work.

415 IR: OK. OK. And that was two and a half weeks ago, this incident we're
416   dealing with?

417 IE: Yeah. I would, I would say about that. It was right, right when I started.

418 IR: OK. And you remember significant changes after that time?

419 IE: I, I remember that she became more of a cry baby and I said, I kept
420   telling Ann. You know, I said, well, "You take her in" you know. And
421   she's like, "Oh, well, she's coming on the check up" and you know "She's
422   probably" you know, you know "Getting use to the food" and all this
423   and that and. I'm like, "Ann, I believe personally that" you know "some-
424   thing is wrong." You know, what, I didn't really associate it with the fall.
425   You know I just figured that probably she was just not feeling well.

426 IR: But nothing so big you thought she had to go to the emergency room?

427 IE: Um, no but I figured she should go to the regular doctor.

428 IR: Get checked up?

429 IE: Yeah.

430 IR: OK. And she didn't get check up the whole time period?

431 IE: Not to my knowledge, no. Because I remember her son and Ann both
432   were sick.

433 IR: Where does she go to the doctor?

434 IE: I don't even know to tell you the truth.

435 IR: I think you said earlier, you didn't go to the hospital because the
436   baby's dad was going to be there? This isn't your child?

437 IE: No.

438 IR: OK. Is the boy, the two year old, your child?

439 IE: No. Neither one, neither one are my children. No.

440 IR: OK.

441 IE: And that's you know, that's why I just want to reiterate you know, I
442   would never do anything to hurt any child you know. And you know,
443   I just that's why I'm just so shocked that this all came about.

444 IR: Now the baby, you said, had a bruise on the front of her head.

445 IE: It was like very light.

446 IR: Did she have any other injuries that you remember?

447 IE: No. None.

448 IR: Because I was told that she had a scrape on her nose.

449 IE: Oh. OK. Yeah, a scrape on her nose.

450 IR: She did have a scrape on her nose?

451 IE: She did have a scrape on her nose. But that might have been when
452   she did the you know the, you know the, the thing on the thing.

453 IR: The thing on the thing?

454 IE: Yeah you know, the handle.

455 IR: Scraped her nose on the handle?

456 IE: Yeah. Or I might have even done that when I was trying you know 'cause
457   I was trying to protect her. I was just trying to grab her as much as I could.

458 IR: Oh, you might have scraped her?

459 IE: I might have accidentally yeah. 'Cause you know, I, my fingernails you
460   know they're kind of sharp.

461 IR: OK.

462 IE: The scrape, that wasn't of any you know significance.

463 IR: Yeah. That was what I was told. It was just kind of an abrasion.

464 IE: Yeah. That might have been from me trying you know when I was

465   trying to grab her. It just you know I'm, I'm you know now, that I

466   think about it and at the time I'm pretty sure, you know, she proba-

467   bly had to hit her head. 'Cause I, I fell hard. I mean it, it, it dinged me.

468 IR: Did you go to the doctor?

469 IE: No I didn't. It just, you know I, I, what I did after Ann got home, I got,

470   I put some hamburger that we had at the time 'cause we didn't have

471   no ice. And I kept sticking it on my head and back and forth on my arm.

472 IR: But you remember this all pretty clearly?

473 IE: Yeah. Well I, you know, I was, you know, it was in the afternoon.

474 IR: Drunk?

475 IE: No.

476 IR: So you were taking care of the kids so you were sober?

477 IE: Oh yeah. I believe I had just got home from work a couple hours earlier.

478 IR: So you remember this?

479 IE: Yeah.

480 IR: Am I right?

481 IE: Remember what?

482 IR: The incident that's all clear?

483 IE: It's all clear.

484 IR: Today, what time did you guys get up?

485 IE: Um. Today, got up, probably, I got up probably about ten thirty.

486 IR: And Ann?

487 IE: She, well, I know the baby was crying, was crying real heavily this morn-

488   ing too and that's what woke me up. And she, she 'cause she went in to

489   sleep in the kid's room. And I had to go in there and I told her, "Ann" I

490   said, "Your daughter's crying," so it was probably a few minutes after me,

491   you know. She just went like, "Oh" you know. And the baby was crying.

492   I remember too, I, you know, I went in and rubbed her head 'cause she

493   was just, you know, crying and looking up. And uh, you know, Ann had

494   gave her, her pacifier. So I had went back and I was going to lay down.

495   I was like, "No" you know, "I might as well get up." You know, it's already,

496   you know starting to get late. So I went back into the room.

497 IR: OK. Did Ann leave already?

498 IE: No.

499 IR: So it was ten thirty?

500 IE: Yeah. She was still in the room. She was laying on the bed.

501 IR: In the master bedroom?

502 IE: No. In the kid's bedroom.

503 IR: OK. She's in the kid's bedroom.

504 IE: Right.

505 IR: Is the two year old there?

506 IE: No. He's with his father this weekend.

507 IR: OK. So Ann's in the bigger bed in that little bedroom?

508 IE: Right.

509 IR: And so is the baby on the bed with her?

510 IE: No. The baby was in the crib.

511 IR: And where were you?

512 IE: I was in our bedroom.

513 IR: OK. And she gave the baby the pacifier?

514 IE: Yeah.

515 IR: And what happened?

516 IE: OK. And you know that's when she got up and the baby like quit cry-
517   ing. So, like I said, I went to go back to lay down. OK. Um, then I know
518   she, she started crying again and I heard, you know, Ann get up. And
519   that's when I said, "I might as well get up." You know, so I went in
520   there and the baby had her pacifier. And she was, you know, kind of
521   like looking up you know, looking around. You know, so I went in and
522   told her, "Good morning" you know and I rubbed her little head.

523 IR: She smile at you?

524 IE: Yeah. She smiled and you know, you know, you could tell she had her
525   pacifier with the little things coming out.

526 IR: Pretty normal day?

527 IE: And I told Ann, I said, "She's soaking" you know, "She's just sweating."
528   You know, 'cause Ann has a little heater in there. An uh, you know and
529   I took that out to the living room later on but she was just soaking,
530   soaking and sweating.

531 IR: But she was happy because she smiled at you?

532 IE: Yeah. And so you know, she, but she you know, she continued you
533   know, kind of whining a little bit but not bad. And so I told Ann, I said,
534   "I'm going to take her" you know, "Her sweats off because she's" you
535   know, "she's just drenched with sweat." And I told her, "It's hot as hell
536   in this room" you know. So I took off her little sweats you know and
537   you know, laid her back down in the crib.

538 IR: Did you change her?

539 IE: No. I didn't and Ann's like, "Well here, give her to me." So, I said, "Al-
540   right." I gave her to her you know. And, and her and Ann were play-
541   ing but you know, after they were playing a little bit she started cry-
542   ing again. 'Cause I went in, that's when I went into the living room you
543   know, to watch TV and that's when she went in you know, and made
544   her, her bottle. You know and uh, then she went back and I, I don't
545   know if she gave her you know, how much of the bottle may have. It's
546   really big you know, 'cause I was watching TV. And I went in there and
547   I could just hear Margaret, telling Margaret, "What do you want?" You
548   know, you know, 'cause I could hear the baby just like crying. It wasn't
549   like a significant cry but, it just, like the cry that I'd been hearing for
550   the last couple of weeks. You know, like I don't, I don't, I don't know
551   how to explain it. Like, you know, she's, she's you know hurting or
552   something was wrong. I don't know, I just. It was just very weird. And
553   then that's when got the phone call from her mom you know. She got
554   the phone call from her mom and she, she had called the bank. And
555   she was pissed. You know she was cussing at the bank, you know, per-
556   son. And uh, I know she grabbed Margaret and she ran, you know, laid
557   her in the crib. You know and I, she said, "Well, I'm going to get her
558   ready 'cause I've got to take her with me." You know, "The bank this
559   and that" you know and, "I don't have my license, this and that." And
560   I'm like, you know, I said, "Well" you know, "It's kind of cold" and I said,
561   "I know the baby's sleepy" you know. I said, you know, "Why don't
562   you" you know, "let her lay down." And uh, so uh, you know, she's like
563   well, you know, "I'm short money in the bank" or the bank something
564   about some of the checks had cleared and she didn't have enough
565   money. So she asked me, "Can you," you know, "can you write me a

566   check" you know, "for twenty-two dollars? And I'll pay you back when
567   I get money from" you know, "my baby's dad or whatever." I said, you
568   know, "Yeah. That's not a problem." You know, I told her to get my
569   check book. So she actually, she wrote the check and the thing. And
570   um, then she was in a haste and I know she had went and she told me
571   well, "Margaret's in her crib." I said, "OK. That's fine" you know. And
572   you know, she just kind of shut the door but she didn't shut it all the
573   way. She left it open like about that much. And then she left.
574 IR: When she was on the phone with the bank, were you in the room with
575   her?
576 IE: Yeah.
577 IR: And was the baby?
578 IE: Uh, for a little bit the baby was in the room.
579 IR: Did you see Ann hurt the baby today?
580 IE: No. I have never seen Ann hurt the baby.
581 IR: She's good with the kids?
582 IE: Good with the kids.
583 IR: So, you don't think that Ann hurt the baby?
584 IE: I don't think, no, I, I, I just, I want to go on the record and say no. I
585   don't believe she would, or ever would hurt the kids.
586 IR: But you didn't see anything?
587 IE: No. I didn't see anything. And like I said she, she, was very, you know,
588   upset with the bank that day.
589 IR: Do you think she took it out on the baby?
590 IE: I don't think so but you know.
591 IR: Did you see her do that?
592 IE: Not when she was in the room with me but then they went into the
593   bedroom.
594 IR: So what happened then before she left?
595 IE: She was just very frustrated and just you know hustling and bustling
596   around.
597 IR: Was the baby screaming?
598 IE: The baby was kind of crying a little bit and then she went and put her
599   in the bed, you know.

600 IR: And then?

601 IE: I heard her whine a little bit you know and then she, she just, Ann
602   came out you know and she started getting her clothes on.

603 IR: Was the baby eating her bottle at that time?

604 IE: I don't know. That I don't know because I wasn't in the room.

605 IR: Was she quiet?

606 IE: Like I said, she was kind of whining a little bit.

607 IR: So she wasn't eating the bottle?

608 IE: I don't think so. I, I really don't know. I wasn't in the bedroom.

609 IR: OK. But I'm trying to remember. You said that Ann fixed the bottle for
610   the baby.

611 IE: This was, this was earlier.

612 IR: OK.

613 IE: When I was watching TV. So I figure she probably did you know when
614   she took her in the bedroom.

615 IR: When you went in later. And you wrote in your statement, you've al-
616   ready told me that you went in later because you heard her fussing,
617   she hadn't eaten all the bottle?

618 IE: No. There was still some there.

619 IR: Because you put the bottle back up and left.

620 IE: Right.

621 IR: When you put the bottle in was she eating?

622 IE: She, she was sucking on it more or less like playing with it.

623 IR: Oh. OK.

624 IE: I really can't, I don't know if she's you know 'cause usually it's like when
625   you give her, her pacifier she'll like put it in her mouth you know and
626   push it in and out a little bit. You know but you know she had quieted
627   down but she was crying so I did that you know. And I figure well, I'll
628   go in here so she'll go back to sleep.

629 IR: Right.

630 IE: So I don't know if she started drinking it or not.

631 IR: But she wasn't freaking out or anything?

632 IE: Not at that particular moment.

633 IR: OK. Alright, so when Ann left, who all was in the house today?

634 IE: It was just me and the baby.

635 IR: And who came over while Ann was gone?

636 IE: Um, nobody. There was just a lot of people hustling you know around
637   outside.

638 IR: But nobody was in the house?

639 IE: No.

640 IR: Just you.

641 IE: Just me.

642 IR: And did Ann come home before you had to call 911?

643 IE: No.

644 IR: When did she get home?

645 IE: She got there like a little bit after the paramedics. A few minutes after.

646 IR: After?

647 IE: Yeah.

648 IR: OK.

649 IE: And everything was just happening so quick.

650 IR: Was today the first time you saw the baby spit up blood?

651 IE: First, no. I had seen her one other time. We were, it was ah, I don't
652   know this was it's already been a while back. Um, but I know we were
653   going to go to the movies one night. And it was actually, I think it was
654   the second day she had gave her cereal. Put cereal in her milk. Uh, and
655   she you know we were going to go to the movies and you know. And
656   Ann had gave her, her bottle and uh I the next thing I know the baby
657   she just, she started crying real hard again, you know. So I kind of
658   lifted on the back and she had, she was bleeding you know from right
659   here. And you know so I was like I tried to wipe it up and I was yelling,
660   "Ann, what's" you know "what's going on?" She's like, "Why's my
661   daughter, why's my daughter bleeding?" I said, "I don't know." You
662   know I said, "You just gave her the bottle a little bit ago" and you
663   know, I said, I was 'cause I was setting there fussing with the radio.
664   'Cause the radio in the car it works sometimes, sometimes it doesn't.
665   So I was trying to get the radio fixed. You know to see if we could get
666   the radio to work so you know so you could listen to the movie in the
667   car. And that was, that was, that was the only other time. But I know,

668   I remember today specifically today when Ann was at the hospital, she
669   told me, you know, I, she goes, "I guess I should have figured some-
670   thing was wrong. " She goes, "When the other day" she goes, "she
671   must have thrown up blood." She goes, "But I thought it was juice." And
672   I'm like, "Well, why didn't you tell me that?" You know, "Why didn't you
673   tell me that something has been going on?"
674 IR: When did you talk to her from the hospital?
675 IE: Um, all day until roughly about three-thirty.
676 IR: OK. Did you talk to her after three-thirty?
677 IE: No.
678 IR: Never?
679 IE: Just until she paged me like uh, probably about eight-thirty, eight-
680   forty-five. Somewhere around there. And then she tried to tell me, "I've
681   been paging you all day." I'm like, "You didn't page me all day because
682   this is the first time that anything came up with your code" you know?
683 IR: What paging service do you have?
684 IE: Acmenet.
685 IR: OK.
686 IE: No wait, I have, it's not. It's Acme Communication. I'm sorry.
687 IR: What kind of pager is it?
688 IE: Just a little bravo.
689 IR: Voice mail?
690 IE: Yeah. Voice mail and you know, regular. And uh.
691 IR: So there'll be a record that you didn't get any pages?
692 IE: Yeah. There would, there would, there, I mean, you know, I did erase
693   my pages 'cause.
694 IR: But, we can get them from the computer.
695 IE: There is no pages from her at all. And also, I gave her my cell phone
696   so she could call me. I told her, "Call me" 'cause I you know, "I want to
697   know what was going on." You know, I was just, you know.
698 IR: So tell me about the conversation this evening?
699 IE: The, the conversation this evening was, was very weird. I mean like I
700   said I was you know pretty you know intoxicated kind of. But I still re-
701   member. You know, she's like, "Hi. How're you doing or what're you

702   doing?" I said, just, you know, "Sitting at Mickey's house." And she's
703   like, "Who's Mickey? I've never heard about Mickey." I said, well, you
704   know, "He just" you know "lives a couple doors down from Mary." You
705   know, "I've known him" you know, "for a long time" you know. "I just
706   went over to see if my sister was you know, was at Mary's house. And
707   nobody was there and it just happened that Mickey was there" you
708   know. "So Mickey, we went and started drinking a few beers." And
709   she's like, "Well how come I've never heard about Mickey?" I'm like,
710   you know "I don't know," you know, "It's no big deal." "Well who else
711   is there with you?" I said, "Mike." "Well who's Mike?" "That's David's
712   dad. That's Mary's son's dad." And she's like, "Oh." And she's like, well
713   like, I, I, I believe, something to the effect that, "are you having a good
714   time?" And I'm like, "No, not really." You know, you know, "Just get-
715   ting buzzed." 'Cause you know I was just, you know today was just a
716   very, a very weird day you know. And I just wanted to kind of not ac-
717   tually put it to the back of your mind but I don't know how to say you
718   know. It just, kinda try to relax a little bit. 'Cause I been so up tight all
719   day. And she's like, "Oh. That's nice." You know. She goes, "Consider-
720   ing that my daughter's passed away." And I'm just, I'm just like, "What
721   do you mean?" You know, "You're kidding right?" "No I'm not." And
722   then she just started trying to tell me, "Well why don't you tell me ex-
723   actly what happened?" And I told her, "I've told you what happened.
724   I wrote a statement of what happened." And she's like, "Well, did you
725   put in that statement about the fall from a couple weeks ago?" And
726   I'm like, "Well, no because it was a statement of what happened
727   today," you know. And she's just like, "Well why don't you just tell me
728   again what happened?" And I told her, "What are you trying to do?
729   Are you trying to get me to admit to something that I said I did do?"
730   But I told her that I didn't do you know. Because I know I was intoxi-
731   cated but I remember saying that and, and I'm like, "I'm not going to
732   admit to anything that I didn't do because I didn't do anything, Ann."
733   I told her, "I told you exactly what happened. I wrote a statement
734   about what happened. And that's what happened" you know. And I
735   told her, "I just, I feel bad." She goes, "Well don't try to tell me that you

736 understand this." And I say, "OK. I'm not going to say that I understand
737 because I don't. I know if I would lose my son, I would probably feel
738 horrendous, really bad." But, you know I told her, "I feel bad enough
739 as it is," you know. And uh, and then she just started going on and I
740 said, "Oh. So, well, I guess you don't want to be with me no more."
741 And she said, "No. Never again." She said something about, "I have to
742 worry about putting this behind me," or something like that. "I don't
743 need to worry about a relationship." I said, "Alright. That's fine." And
744 then she said a couple other things. And I said well, just, "whatever."
745 I said, "I'll just," you know, "I'll talk to you later" and I hung up. And
746 that was the end of the conversation.
747 IR: You didn't say, "Fuck the police, I'm not going to go on Monday"?
748 IE: No, I didn't say, "Fuck the police." I told her, I remember I told her, she
749 said, "You going to be there Monday?" And I said, "No. I'm not going
750 to go Monday." Because she was trying to make me you know sound
751 like I was doing something bad, you know. I don't remember saying,
752 "Fuck the police." And I don't think I would say, "Fuck the police."
753 IR: I think we had that call made from up here in this office.
754 IE: OK. But I don't think I said, "Fuck the police" though. I probably said
755 something about, "I want go on Monday."
756 IR: Why wouldn't you go on Monday?
757 IE: Because she was pissing me off. Trying to make it sound like I did
758 something.
759 IR: Well her baby just died.
760 IE: I know but she doesn't gotta come after me. I mean, I just totally felt,
761 felt bad. Yeah. I was gonna go on Monday. You know, I was just, I had
762 just talked to my sister you know. I got a hold of her at the house and
763 I told her what happened. And I told her I got to go there Monday. You
764 know I told her, I got to make you know I had to make arrangements
765 for my job. To get off you know in time to go to that you know. 'Cause
766 I had to, I'm you know supposed to be to work at three o'clock in the
767 morning on Monday.
768 IR: About eleven forty-five you were driving by the house. Tell me about
769 that.

770 IE: Just, I wanted to just go see if Ann was there so we could talk.

771 IR: Why didn't you stop?

772 IE: I just, I just, you know didn't want to stop.

773 IR: Why?

774 IE: Just didn't. I didn't know. I figured you guys were probably talking to
775   Ann.

776 IR: Well you could see us. We were standing outside.

777 IE: Well I yeah. But I couldn't see inside.

778 IR: No.

779 IE: I didn't know what was going on inside.

780 IR: Nothing was going on. Why didn't you stop and see?

781 IE: Well, I just figured I was just going to drive by 'cause I wanted to talk
782   to Ann on a one on one basis.

783 IR: Oh. You didn't want to talk to the police?

784 IE: No. It wasn't that I didn't want to talk to the police. I wanted to talk to
785   Ann and you know tell her that I felt very bad and you know how very
786   sorry I am you know.

787 IR: Why are you sorry?

788 IE: Because her daughter died you know. And I don't know if there is any-
789   more that I could have done you know. I, you know, I called 911. I did
790   what the guy told me you know. And I just, I keep playing it back in
791   my mind. Could I have done anything different, you know?

792 IR: Now you said that the baby threw up blood.

793 IE: Yeah.

794 IR: You went in and got a towel and cleaned it up.

795 IE: She spit up blood.

796 IR: Right.

797 IE: She spit up. So I wiped it up.

798 IR: Where did that towel go?

799 IE: It was in the washer with the other stuff. Like I said 'cause I didn't want,
800   you know I didn't want Ann to see all that stuff. 'Cause I knew she
801   would freak out. And she goes, I mean she goes hysterical I mean
802   when her little son you know he's playing and he falls just ah, she's you
803   know just, just extremely hyperactive.

804 IR: You didn't think she was going to freak out when an ambulance took
805   her baby to the hospital?
806 IE: Oh yeah. But I didn't want her to you know see all that. Then she
807   would really, really, really go into hysteria you know.
808 IR: You were trying to protect her?
809 IE: Yeah. I figured she needed to be at least somewhat calm you know.
810 IR: So the paramedics took the baby out to the ambulance?
811 IE: Yeah.
812 IR: That's when you put the sheet in the washer?
813 IE: Yeah.
814 IR: You didn't go out with the paramedics to the ambulance?
815 IE: No. 'Cause they told they just they said, "Everybody out of the way"
816   you know. They just said, "Move."
817 IR: Seems to me like you're more concerned with the sheet than the baby.
818 IE: No. I was already, I was, as soon as they grabbed the baby you know
819   what I'm saying, I, I just I was like, "Oh God. Ann gonna just" you know
820   "Ann's gonna freak" you know. So I just stood there and you know
821   there were just like people gathering around and they told everybody
822   to get out of the way you know. And then as soon as Ann came in I
823   talked to her. I hugged her. She went out there and the paramedics
824   told her to get out of the way.
825 IR: Then what happened to the sheet?
826 IE: And then the police officer came. And I, she asked me you know,
827   "What was here?" And I told her. And she asked me to show it to her
828   and I got it for her.
829 IR: And the towel was in there too?
830 IE: Yeah.
831 IR: You got the towel out of there too?
832 IE: No. She, she, she just got the sheet. I told her about the towel.
833 IR: Where did the towel go?
834 IE: It was in the washer. I washed it with my uniforms today.
835 IR: Oh. You did wash the towel?
836 IE: Yeah. 'Cause I was gonna, I washed my uniforms you know.
837 IR: But there's no other towels with blood on it in your house?

838 IE: No. There was just, just that. I mean it wasn't, it wasn't much. It was
839   just like the same kind of stuff that was on the sheet.
840 IR: OK.
841 IE: Just, you know it was just very how would you say, just very, very
842   strange. I was just like, "Oh. My God" you know. And I just you know
843   I thought I would wipe her up and you know. I figured you know I fig-
844   ured I had scratched her. That's what I figured it was from.
845 IR: OK. Anything else that we should know right now that you can think of?
846 IE: No.

Appendix B

The Final Eighteen Minutes of the Homicide Interview

Note: Carefully read the following transcript of the last eighteen minutes of the interview. Throughout this transcript you will see the abbreviations IR and IE. IR represents statements made or questions asked by the interviewer, IE represents those made by interviewee.

847 IR: OK. Now Andrew, I'm going to lay this on the line to you.

848 IE: OK.

849 IR: You've been talking now for almost an hour, forty minutes.

850 IE: Well, I was just trying to be as cooperative …

851 IR: No. And I appreciate that. There's going to be an autopsy tomorrow.
852 And I have already seen the x-rays and the scan. I have a pretty good
853 idea of what happened to the baby. OK. There's been a lot of science
854 done over the years about what injuries cause what to babies. You
855 know what I'm saying?

856 IE: Yeah.

857 IR: We can medically say. We can date bruises, date cuts. We can date
858 breaks in bones.

859 IE: OK.

860 IR: All of these.

861 IE: I don't I don't believe she had anything like that.

862 IR: OK. But we can scientifically do that.

863 IE: Right.

864 IR: OK. And that's going to be done one way or the other. Eventually this
865 is going to go, this situation, the whole deal, three days is going to go
866 to a district attorney. OK. And the district attorney is going to sit down
867 and listen to all the facts. And you've told your side of the story. We've
868 got Ann's story. We've got the autopsy. So we've got a lot of different

869   stories. OK. And if several of the stories match and one of them doesn't,
870   how do you think the DA is going to view that?
871 IE: I don't know. The thing that I'm telling you, you know, is true.
872 IR: OK. And that's what I want.
873 IE: The fall is, you know, that, that happened.
874 IR: OK. And I want you to tell the truth. I don't want you to tell me any-
875   thing that didn't happen.
876 IE: That's, that's what happened.
877 IR: OK. The DA is going to make a decision that can affect the rest of your
878   life.
879 IE: Right.
880 IR: Because they're going to decide whether to charge you with murder,
881   whether to charge you with child abuse resulting in death, whether
882   to charge you with negligence, whether to charge you with man-
883   slaughter, second degree murder or maybe nothing. See there are a
884   lot of options out there for the district attorney.
885 IE: Right.
886 IR: Now, first degree murder carries what? Do you know?
887 IE: No.
888 IR: That's a life sentence. That's mandatory life. We can go all the way down
889   to negligence which carries a few years. Or even child abuse, misde-
890   meanor child abuse which carries you know it's a misdemeanor term. OK.
891 IE: OK.
892 IR: OK. So it's a very important decision that the DA is going to make. OK.
893   Whatever decision he makes it's going to go onto court. Right? Unless
894   they don't charge you with anything.
895 IE: Right.
896 IR: OK. It's going to go onto court probably and there'll be a case. And
897   eventually that case will go before twelve people in a jury.
898 IE: Right.
899 IR: Right. And those twelve people are going to get to see this tape. They
900   are going to get to see what you said. How that you held the baby and
901   all those kinds of things.
902 IE: That's, that's totally fine.

903 IR: Right.

904 IE: 'Cause everything that I told you is true.

905 IR: OK.

906 IE: And that's, that's the way it happened.

907 IR: OK. And here's what I want to tell you, Andrew.

908 IE: OK.

909 IR: OK. What you are telling me doesn't add up. And so what they're
910   going to hear is just that.

911 IE: What do you mean it doesn't add up?

912 IR: I'm going to explain that to you.

913 IE: OK.

914 IR: What I want you to think about is this. If you were one of those twelve
915   people and somebody else was sitting there in front of you, would you
916   rather hear from them, "Ah, hey, it was an accident. I didn't mean for
917   it to happen this way. I lost my temper. I'm not that kind of a guy. I
918   would never intentionally hurt a child. I might have just got frustrated
919   for a second."

920 IE: No.

921 IR: No. I'm just telling you. I want you to think about it.

922 IE: I don't get frustrated.

923 IR: I want you to think about it.

924 IE: OK.

925 IR: Because if you don't, if you hear this, what you've told me today.

926 IE: Right.

927 IR: And then all the physical evidence that we have and witness state-
928   ments that we have and the neighbor's statements that we have had
929   come in and they don't support anything that you said, and you were
930   the only person who was alone with that child.

931 IE: Uh, Um.

932 IR: And they're thinking to themselves, "I'll bet he meant for this to hap-
933   pen." I mean, maybe they'll say to themselves, "You know what? This
934   guy wanted to get rid of this kid because he didn't want Ann sharing
935   that kid's attention." If they, if you leave it up to those people to try
936   and decide what you were thinking.

937 IE: OK. I'm listening but now that you have said that. I know that that's

938   something that stems from Ann. 'Cause she always tells me that I'm

939   jealous of her. And I'm like, you know, "What, what do you mean?"

940 IR: So Andrew, what I'm trying to tell you is if this was an accident.

941 IE: It was.

942 IR: And if you didn't intend for this to end up like it did today, you need

943   to say that now. This is your chance. Because I can tell you this. I want

944   to tell you this. I saw the x-rays.

945 IE: OK.

946 IR: I saw the scan. That injury, the child could not have lived two weeks

947   period. And I know, let me tell you this, especially in children, bone

948   grows very fast.

949 IE: Right.

950 IR: Babies heal very fast. If that was a two week old injury.

951 IE: Uh, uh.

952 IR: You would see that. I mean it's as clear as day. There's no doctor in the

953   world that wouldn't get on the stand and testify.

954 IE: But, but there's no way that I mean 'cause I didn't touch the child today

955   other than that. And I swear, I, I put that on everything you know.

956 IR: OK. I'll tell you what the doctors told me today.

957 IE: OK.

958 IR: That baby's head impacted against a hard surface today.

959 IE: Today?

960 IR: Today.

961 IE: There's, there's no way it could have impacted today.

962 IR: Well then Andrew, I guess everybody's going to have to try and sec-

963   ond guess you. If you won't tell us. You won't explain why it happened

964   the way it did.

965 IE: I would explain to you if it happened any other way.

966 IR: I don't think that you will.

967 IE: I swear to God I would. There is no other, there is nothing that I did to

968   that child.

969 IR: Does science lie?

970 IE: I don't know.

971 IR: No.

972 IE: I don't believe it does.

973 IR: No. Because they're facts. The facts are going to show that that injury
974   occurred today.

975 IE: But, how could that injury have occurred today?

976 IR: That's what I want to know. I wasn't there. You were the only one there
977   based on your own statement.

978 IE: There is no way that that injury occurred today.

979 IR: Andrew, we have neighbors who hear some stuff going on over there.
980   I tell you.

981 IE: They probably heard me panicking to death calling 911.

982 IR: I want you to know that you have a chance here to explain things. And
983   maybe have it come out a lot different than first degree murder. Maybe
984   you have an anger management problem. Maybe you just need some
985   counseling when it comes to dealing with kids. Maybe you're a pro-
986   bationary kind of person. You know, you got a good job. You got a nice
987   house. You take care of things. If this wasn't intentional, I mean I don't
988   think you picked this baby up and threw it against the wall.

989 IE: I, I didn't pick the baby up and throw it against the wall.

990 IR: But Andrew.

991 IE: I don't know.

992 IR: There's no reason not to tell these people the truth so that they can un-
993   derstand what was going through your mind. Don't make people guess.

994 IE: OK. I, I was just trying, trying to think of any reason that it is.

995 IR: OK. I've had some cases before where people get a little frustrated.
996   I've been around a lot of babies. They cry. They get on your nerves.
997   They bug you. You get tired of it. You think, "I shouldn't be taking care
998   of this baby. This isn't my baby. This isn't my job." Maybe some peo-
999   ple shake it like this and put it down. They don't intend to cause any
1000   injury to the child. They didn't mean for anything to happen to the
1001   baby. Maybe they put the baby down hard in the crib and while they
1002   did that the baby's head strikes the edge of the crib. Things like that
1003   happen. That happens to people.

1004 IE: OK.

1005 IR: Babies are very delicate, little things.

1006 IE: They are. They're very delicate.

1007 IR: So little things can make big things happen. I mean you don't have
1008   to throw a kid against the wall to hurt them. Right? But when the
1009   doctors go in there and they say that the injury occurred on Octo-
1010   ber seventeenth.

1011 IE: I just don't see how that injury could have occurred today. I just …

1012 IR: I'm telling you Andrew that injury occurred on October seventeenth.

1013 IE: I'm just, I'm just trying to think back and I don't see.

1014 IR: The injury occurred from an impact on that baby's head into a hard
1015   surface. Did you go like this?

1016 IE: No. I didn't.

1017 IR: Well then show me what happened. Explain it so that these people
1018   will know.

1019 IE: The only, the only thing that happened today is like I said. When I was
1020   running around you know with the 911, trying to call 911. I was look-
1021   ing for the phone.

1022 IR: Um Uh.

1023 IE: OK. And I know when she was kind of you know kind of getting how
1024   would you say, getting kind of limp. I did you know try to brush a lit-
1025   tle bit of water on her, you know in the sink.

1026 IR: Where was that?

1027 IE: In the bathroom, you know.

1028 IR: Show me that. Show me how you did it.

1029 IE: I just you know, I, I had her like this and I reached over to turn on the
1030   faucet you know just try to slap a little bit of water on her, you know.

1031 IR: This was before 911?

1032 IE: This was right, right before.

1033 IR: And did she hit her head then?

1034 IE: I don't know. I know I was kind of panicking.

1035 IR: Do you think she did?

1036 IE: I don't know. I was just, I was so panicking at that point.

1037 IR: Did you drop her?

1038 IE: No. I didn't drop her.

1039 IR: Because this isn't a little hit.

1040 IE: No.

1041 IR: This is a fracture like that.

1042 IE: I didn't drop her. I swear to God I didn't drop her. And I, you know.

1043 IR: Did you throw her?

1044 IE: No. I didn't throw her. I'm not that, I'm not that way. You know, I know
1045   it's not up to you to believe me. But I swear, you know, I'm not, I'm
1046   not that kind of person. You could ask anybody that knows me. I'm
1047   not that type of person, you know. I didn't throw her, you know. I was
1048   just, I was panicking you know because she was just, you know, she
1049   was coughing, you know. And I just, I, I don't know. I'm trying, I'm try-
1050   ing to think back. Everything's happened so fast.

1051 IR: I want to tell you what I think happened.

1052 IE: OK.

1053 IR: And as a guy I can understand this. OK.

1054 IE: OK.

1055 IR: I think you were tired. You had to get up before you wanted to. You
1056   were watching TV. Ann leaves you with the baby. You didn't really
1057   want to watch the baby but whatever. She had to go take care of her
1058   business. OK. So she's in there, the baby's in there. The baby's eating.
1059   And then the baby starts crying, whatever. You go in there and you
1060   put the baby's bottle back in. Fine, the baby's eating. You go back and
1061   watch TV. You just sit down. You just get settled down to watch TV
1062   and the baby starts crying again. And that can be very frustrating. It
1063   can be very frustrating. And you walk in and you go, "What is wrong
1064   with you?" You pick up the baby, OK. Because you don't know what's
1065   wrong with the baby. It's not your baby. OK.

1066 IE: I, I.

1067 IR: Listen to me, because I can understand this. OK.

1068 IE: OK.

1069 IR: And you were a little frustrated and maybe you put the baby down
1070   too hard. Maybe you picked the baby up like this a little bit. And the
1071   baby accidentally hit its head. You put the baby down. And then you

1072   tried to help the baby. Because you weren't intending to go in there
1073   and hurt the baby. That was not on your mind.
1074 IE: I would never hurt a baby intentionally.
1075 IR: But maybe accidentally, Andrew.
1076 IE: Maybe accidentally but I don't, I don't recall.
1077 IR: Andrew. I don't recall doesn't hold up in court. These people want to
1078   know what got you to the point you were at. That's all. I want to un-
1079   derstand. I want to understand the frustration.
1080 IE: I don't know. I didn't, I wasn't frustrated.
1081 IR: Andrew. I know you were and you know you were. And I can see it.
1082 IE: But, I didn't, I.
1083 IR: I know you didn't mean to do it. But let me explain how you did it so
1084   that they can make a good decision. Don't make people base their
1085   decision on this lie that you told a few minutes ago. You know what
1086   I believe? I believe you did fall with the baby two weeks ago.
1087 IE: I did fall with the baby.
1088 IR: But I don't think the baby's been acting much different. And I don't I
1089   don't think the baby suffered any injury that caused her to die today.
1090   And I don't think you do either.
1091 IE: I believe that the baby did suffer an accident. And I don't, I don't.
1092 IR: And do you believe that the baby got an injury on the back of its head
1093   that caused it to die today?
1094 IE: I don't know.
1095 IR: I'm asking you.
1096 IE: I, I hit my head very hard that day.
1097 IR: Andrew. Let me tell you something. That's not it. She didn't. She didn't.
1098   And I can prove it. And if you want a jury to think, "Oh well. This guy
1099   is just trying to lie his way out of it by saying it was an accident." No.
1100   You know what I would want a jury to do? I would want a jury to
1101   know what I was thinking, what I was feeling and what really hap-
1102   pened. Because maybe it is not first degree murder.
1103 IE: It's not murder because I didn't.
1104 IR: Andrew. Andrew.

1105 IE: I didn't murder, murder the child. Well, I didn't mean, I, the part about
1106   her choking and everything with the blood, that's, that's the truth.

1107 IR: So tell me what else.

1108 IE: That's true. I did, I did get her. And I did kind of shake her.

1109 IR: Show me.

1110 IE: 'Cause you know, she was, she was choking. And I grabbed her
1111   mouth, you know. And, and I did stick my finger in there because she
1112   was choking, you know. And after that's when the blood came out.
1113   And I got her and I was like, "Margaret, Margaret" you know, 'cause
1114   she was, you know, she was just going limp on me already, you know.

1115 IR: OK.

1116 IE: And then.

1117 IR: Andrew. Andrew. Before you go any further. Before you do some-
1118   thing that you don't want to do. OK. There's people that I talk to that
1119   what they need is not prison. They don't need to be locked up with
1120   four thousand other guys in a cage. What they need is help.

1121 IE: OK.

1122 IR: Maybe you're a guy that needs help. But, I've never once see a guy
1123   that needs help that didn't ask for it.

1124 IE: Well, can I get some help?

1125 IR: You have to tell the truth. You have to show me that it was a mistake,
1126   that it was an accident. You have to show me exactly what you did.
1127   It's going to match what we find in the coroner's report tomorrow.
1128   And I can talk to the district attorney about you needing help. If that's
1129   what you need try to show us.

1130 IE: I did. I, I shook her.

1131 IR: Because you were angry.

1132 IE: I was, I was, I was scared.

1133 IR: A guy doesn't need help for being scared.

1134 IE: I was scared though.

1135 IR: But a guy doesn't need help for being scared. A guy needs help for
1136   being angry. Maybe you have an anger management problem.
1137   Maybe you need a little counseling when it comes to parenting. But
1138   you have got to tell me that.

1139 IE: Just, whew. I didn't mean to hurt her at all. But she wouldn't, you
1140   know, she was choking and fidgeting.
1141 IR: That was after, I know.
1142 IE: She did choke too.
1143 IR: I know but that was after. Let's start at the beginning. Tell me the
1144   truth so I can tell the DA the truth. Let's do it right.
1145 IE: OK. I just, after I shook her I put her back in the crib.
1146 IR: Start from the beginning.
1147 IE: OK.
1148 IR: You're on the couch.
1149 IE: Yeah. I'm on the couch and she started crying.
1150 IR: OK.
1151 IE: OK. So I went in there and I just, you know, I, I, I did give her, her bot-
1152   tle. And she just, she just wouldn't stop crying. So I grabbed her and
1153   I and I shook her.
1154 IR: Show me.
1155 IE: I just, you know, I was just like, "Margaret" you know just "Please" you
1156   know "Quit crying."
1157 IR: Show me.
1158 IE: I'm showing you.
1159 IR: You're frustrated.
1160 IE: Yeah. You know.
1161 IR: No. I don't want to be mean Andrew. But this doesn't cause an injury.
1162 IE: OK.
1163 IR: Show me.
1164 IE: OK. I picked her up.
1165 IR: Stand up and show me. She's in the crib.
1166 IE: I just, I picked her up.
1167 IR: OK. This is the crib.
1168 IE: Yeah. I picked her up. And I first, I grabbed her. I said, "Margaret" you
1169   know "What's wrong? Why are you crying?" And she wouldn't quit
1170   crying. And it just out, out and I'm like, "Margaret, Margaret. Please,
1171   please quit crying" you know "Please." I didn't know what to do, you
1172   know. Just, "Please quit crying" you know. And I grabbed her head.

1173 IR: Did you really hold the back of her head?

1174 IE: Yeah.

1175 IR: Did you shake her?

1176 IE: I shook her. I shook her. I shook her hard.

1177 IR: Show me because you are frustrated.

1178 IE: I'm showing you. I shook her hard.

1179 IR: That might cause an injury.

1180 IE: I didn't, I didn't mean to though.

1181 IR: Then what happened?

1182 IE: And then I got her and I said, "I'm so sorry Margaret."

1183 IR: No. How did her head get hurt then?

1184 IE: That I don't know.

1185 IR: No. Andrew. You're going back.

1186 IE: OK. When I was shaking her, I hit her back of the head on the crib.

1187 IR: Show me.

1188 IE: You know. Because the crib is up here like this and I was shaking her.

1189 IR: So make that the back of the crib.

1190 IE: Can I make this the back of the crib?

1191 IR: Sure.

1192 IE: And I was shaking her and hit like that.

1193 IR: OK.

1194 IE: And I was like, "Oh. Shit."

1195 IR: And then what?

1196 IE: I just kind of freaked out.

1197 IR: Right

1198 IE: And I was like, "I'm sorry Margaret. I'm sorry." And I laid her back down.

1199 IR: Show me.

1200 IE: You know. I laid her back down.

1201 IR: And then after?

1202 IE: She just started crying harder and she started choking.

1203 IR: Different? Was she crying different?

1204 IE: Just harder. And then she started gasping.

1205 IR: Right then?

1206 IE: Yeah.

1207 IR: What did you do?

1208 IE: I, I you know, I just I kind of lifted her mouth. I was like, "Oh no. What
1209   did I do?" You know, just you know I didn't know. You know so that's
1210   when I did do that finger sweep thing. And then that's when she
1211   started, she started with the blood.

1212 IR: Right.

1213 IE: I feel so bad.

1214 IR: I know you do.

1215 IE: I don't want people to hate me though. 'Cause I'm not that way.

1216 IR: You just made a mistake.

1217 IE: I made a fucking terrible mistake.

1218 IR: You were frustrated, tired of the screaming.

1219 IE: I was just so tired 'cause she wouldn't stop. I didn't mean to do it. The
1220   hitting her head on the crib when I was shaking her, that, that was a
1221   total accident.

1222 IR: Yeah.

1223 IE: I swear to God. I don't want people to hate me.

1224 IR: You didn't go in there intending to hurt her.

1225 IE: No. I didn't, I wouldn't I would never hurt her.

1226 IR: You were frustrated.

1227 IE: Yeah. The thing I told you about the falling, that's, that's the honest
1228   truth.

1229 IR: I believe you.

Appendix C

Persuasive Interview Strategic Plan

Note: This form may serve as a template to assist in planning for the interview.

1. My objective for this interview is to _____

   _____

   _____

2. I plan to achieve this objective by: _____

   _____

   _____

3. I anticipate the following challenges regarding meeting my objective: __

   _____

   _____

   _____

4. In response to those challenges I plan to: _____

   _____

   _____

   _____

5. The frames that would be most conducive to this type of interview would likely be:

   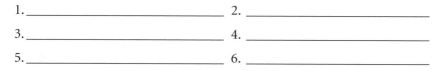

   1._____   2._____

   3._____   4._____

   5._____   6._____

6. The vocabulary most conducive to these frames include: _____

_____

_____

7. The pronouns that I want to emphasize are:

1. _____ 2. _____ 3. _____ 4. _____ 5. _____

8. The pronouns that I want to avoid are:

1. _____ 2. _____ 3. _____ 4. _____ 5. _____

Notes

Chapter One

1. Reber, Arthur S. and Reber, Emily, *The Penguin Dictionary of Psychology*. Third Edition, Penguin Books, 2001, p. 529.
2. *Encarta Dictionary*: English (North American)
3. Reber, Arthur S. and Reber, Emily, *The Penguin Dictionary of Psychology*. Third Edition, Penguin Books, 2001, p. 783.
4. Ibid., p. 86.
5. Ibid., p. 63.
6. Ibid., p. 284.
7. Ibid., p. 285.

Chapter Two

8. Rabon, Don, *Investigative Discourse Analysis*. Carolina Academic Press, 1994.
9. Ibid.
10. Ibid.
11. Ibid.
12. Ibid.
13. Ibid.
14. Ibid.
15. Ibid.
16. Ibid.

Chapter Three

17. Rabon, Don, *Investigative Discourse Analysis*. Carolina Academic Press, 1994.
18. Ibid.
19. Ibid.
20. Ibid.
21. Ibid.

Chapter Four

22. Rabon, Don, *Investigative Discourse Analysis.* Carolina Academic Press, 1994.